Evan's Earthly Adventure

by

Mark Holofcener

BeyondTime Books
Groton, Massachusetts

BeyondTime Books, Groton, MA 01450

Printed in the United States of America

Acknowledgments

Thanks to Ellen Beth Lande for her clear thinking, her valuable insights, and her ability to unstick me when I was stuck.

Thanks to Jamie Kulesz for her invaluable help in editing my book. Lots of red pens used on this project.

Thanks to Nancy and Ryan for their patience and understanding and their support.

Thanks to Ken Godowski for his permission to use the cover and back photos

Thanks to everyone who read the numerous series of rough drafts and gave me valuable insights, some of which I actually listened to.

Thanks to Evan's friends who were such a large part of the book.

And also *thanks* to our friends who helped us when we needed to talk and listened to our ongoing drama.

Thanks to Prem Rawat who showed me how to find what I was looking for

Most of all, I thank Evan for his courage and inspiration

Authors Note

Is life an adventure from the beginning to the end, or are adventures only for children? Is it foolish to think of having adventures throughout our life, relegating all the fun and the mystery of finding *the* answers to others? Has the innocence in us that was alive in abundance when we were young seemingly disappeared, along with the sense of excitement about living each day? No—it's still there, waiting to be discovered. It might be hidden, but it's there, waiting to be realized and put into use, transforming our lives into that very sense of wonderment we frolicked in as children. Only this time, it is adventure with a purpose, and the excitement is the discovery of life itself. This isn't a theory or a nice thought. This is real.

As this story unfolded I was surprised at the twists and turns that presented themselves to me and I understood my need to be open to where I was being led. The end result is nothing that resembled my original idea, which I think is great. I decided to separate information by indicating a journal entry date, as that is the only way I could chronicle the events that unfolded.

There is a journey that is being described, and one that can also be had by the reader. There are a few requirements however, and I would ask you to simply suspend your beliefs and ideas, for the moment, and just "*listen*" to the words as if you were very, very thirsty, and the words were leading you to water. The words can never be water, but they can point you in the right direction.

Each one of us is on our own earthly journey. This is the chronicle of one young man who completed his.

September 1, 2001

Evan had gone out for a bike ride on his new, full suspension Gary Fisher mountain bike, which Gary Fisher had signed personally. He was wearing his helmet as he always did. He loved that bike, and he loved riding in the rural countryside in Groton, Massachusetts, where we live. It gave him so much pleasure to ride shirtless, with a water pack on his back, so proud of his amazing physique he worked so hard to perfect over the summer.

Bike riding provided Evan with the joy of feeling the wind against his face, and the opportunity to test himself against his ideal image of the perfect ride, and to gain strength for the upcoming hockey season. He spent hours riding every day this past summer, usually on the miles of trails surrounding our house, or on the rail-trail which was being constructed nearby. He would come home sweaty, exhausted, and dirty, typically with a huge smile on his face. *"awesome ride"* he'd say when asked how the ride was.

September 1st was a beautiful summer day. School had started only two days earlier and Evan was elated to be back with his friends and his new-found determination to succeed. He cleaned his room, organized his folders and notebooks, and inventoried his clothes a week before school started, shocking my wife Nancy and me. He was ready: ready for school, and ready to face all that life had to offer, with passion, joy, determination, and purpose. He was happy—the happiest I had ever known him to be. Evan was at the pinnacle of his life.

My son Evan was killed on September 1, 2001 while riding his mountain bike on the sidewalk by a driver that swerved from the road and struck him while she was under the influence of a combination of prescription drugs. He was killed less than one mile from our home and about 200 yards from his destination: a downhill trail behind the Groton School. The loss was and is so devastating that words are not sufficient to describe it. When people say that they can't imagine the pain and suffering we must feel when our children are no longer with us, they have no idea how right they are. If you were to get a glimpse of the pain and suffering, life would become unbearable, thus it is merciful and right that there are some things that you simply cannot fathom or experience until you have to.

Evan mentioned to some of his friends, in the weeks prior to the accident, that his life was perfect. Evan was a gifted musician (guitarist), an artist, a poet, a writer, a mentor, an honor roll student, a counselor to his friends, a gifted athlete, a great friend, and a wonderful son and brother. He was a true renaissance child. A local paper, *The Groton Landmark*, noted in their article about the tragedy, "Groton teen remembered for being an 'Amazing Kid'." Evan was just 13 years old.

Evan had been gone for what seemed like an especially long time, considering the fact that he said he was only going for a short ride. Nancy and I started to get concerned when Evan didn't return home for quite some time. I started searching for him in my car and came upon a police barricade not far from our house. I drove up to the barricade and was not allowed to go any further. I didn't know what the accident was that the police were preventing me from seeing. *"Car accident,"* the officer said. I asked whether a bike was involved but got no answer. I wasn't too alarmed at that point because I thought the accident was between two cars, but nonetheless I decided to investigate further.

I raced home in the car and got my bike. I zoomed through the police barricade and came upon a scene consisting of lots of police cars and a large crowd of people who were all staring at me. Nobody spoke a word. It was eerily silent. Then I saw my son's mountain bike on the side of the road, his helmet on the ground with a small amount of blood on the inside padding, a smashed utility pole and a pick up truck flipped on its side.

I didn't see Evan anywhere. Time started slowing down and then stood still. I started screaming, *"where is my son, where is my son"*? Silence. No one from the crowd said a word. The silence was deafening.

Finally, a voice from the crowd said, *"your son is dead."*To this day I don't know who the person was that gave me the horrible news.

"NOOOOOOOOOOOOOOOOOOOOOOOOOOOOOOOOOOO" I screamed, as I fell to my knees. *"This can't be. This can't be possible. Not Evan. He CAN'T be dead. This can't be,"* I remember screaming over and over and over and over. At that point I was thinking, *"please God why can't he be badly hurt instead of dead?"* Never in your wildest dreams would you be hoping that your child was injured, and that it would be okay somehow— because it would mean that he wasn't dead. That thought is so chilling to your mind that it can't seem to comprehend the plea.

By the time I arrived at the accident scene, Evan had been dead for an hour or so, having been airlifted to a major hospital after his immediate treatment at our local hospital just down the road from where he was hit. He died en route to the hospital, inside the helicopter. He was taken care of almost instantly by an EMT (emergency medical technician) who lived just across the street from the accident scene. She took great care of Evan within seconds of him being hit, prior to the ambulance coming. It was good to know, in retrospect, that he was well taken care of, although he was unconscious at the time. Still, our hearts felt better knowing he had the best of care at the end, just as he had at the beginning and throughout his life.

Evan had a cell phone with him and we kept calling and calling him earlier in the day when we were starting to get concerned about him, but there was no answer. I guess the EMTs didn't realize that there was a cell phone in his water pack, although the phone was never turned on. Nancy insisted he take it while Evan was racing out of the house that morning, frantically saying he had to leave right then. It was the first time I remembered that Evan didn't have the cell phone turned on. I was watering the lawn at the time and lightly squirted him with the hose just as he was zooming off. He turned around and smiled. His last words to his mother were *"Mom, you're such a Mom."* Evan's first and last spoken word was *"Mom."*

Of all the children in the world, it couldn't be Evan. He was so strong, so smart, so determined, so beautiful, so awesome, so cool, and so full of life. I had just been with him a few hours ago. I was now in the midst of the worst nightmare imaginable, except this one was real; my worst fear in the world has happened. One of my children is dead. It was horrifying beyond description. My mind was racing, my heart was beating so fast, and my breath was hard to catch. A huge hole had been ripped through the fabric of my life, my universe. A moment ago seemed like another world, another time; the time before my entire world would be annihilated. The time when my life was normal. I had entered a wormhole, instantly transporting me to another universe, far away and so fast, filled with so much pain and suffering that I never knew existed. My old world, the one in which Evan existed, was literally destroyed. I now exist in a new world, where Evan never was.

Of course I remember Evan. In the new world I feel as though I am an explorer blasted to this lonely existence with no guidance and no feeling about what is right and what is wrong. I feel as if I was a child; everything that I will learn is in the future, and I can't rely upon my old-world intuition or knowledge to help me. I feel utterly alone, and I hurt from a lack of clarity and the pain from being suddenly disassociated with the only life I knew; the world where my whole family was intact. I can only describe my life at this point as a continuing episode of "*The Twilight Zone*," seemingly without end.

Worse than the discovery that was unfolding before me was the realization that I now had to tell my wife Nancy about Evan. She was waiting at home for me to return with news about him. She was still thinking that he was just out for a bike ride, although she was concerned that he had been gone for too long, just as I was before I started searching for him.

I insisted that an ambulance accompany the police car to our house because I feared that Nancy would have a heart attack or stroke and die instantly when she heard about Evan. Six months earlier, Nancy had a mini stroke that paralyzed half her face when she was worried about Evan and his involvement with some neighborhood kids that involved the police. It eventually turned out to be nothing, but that is how connected Nancy was to Evan and concerned for his well-being. I was, of course, also thinking about telling having to tell Ryan that his big brother was dead. How could I possibly do that?

Nancy's love for Evan was incredibly deep, and the bond between them was unusually strong. Now I would have to be the one to give her the news that her beloved Evan was dead. All I can say is that the scene at our house was beyond the imagination to comprehend. Sad beyond all words. Nancy's primal scream was certainly heard in every atom of the universe.

Evan's ten-year old brother Ryan came running from a neighbor's house when he heard his mom screaming. *"What happened?"* he asked. *"Evan's dead,"* I told him. *"Stop joking,"* as if that would be something I would joke about. But from his ten-year-old perspective the thought that his big brother was dead was incomprehensible. Evan was so strong, and he always wore his helmet. *"How could he be hurt if he had his helmet on?"* Ryan asked over and over. Ryan loved, and looked up to his big brother. Now he was gone. *"I hate everything,"* he said, and would continue to say in the ensuing weeks. We couldn't blame him. So did we.

The ambulance that accompanied the police car to our house took Nancy, Ryan and me to the hospital to see if we were okay. We weren't!! During the short agonizing ride, we learned more about the details of Evan's death. All of us were in total, complete shock and disbelief. Thinking about Evan being dead was too much for us to comprehend. It seemed like a dream, and we wished it were. We were to find out differently.

> *"When my son Evan died, the fabric of my world, my family life was ripped apart. Losing a child was my worst fear, one that I didn't allow myself to go near or explore. I could never watch TV or movies whose subject involved abuse of a child or families being destroyed in one way or another: mothers having their kids kidnapped. I can't stand and won't watch people hurting each other (as documented daily in the many forms of media). I didn't understand how, having done everything 'right' that I could lose*

my child. I must be a bad mother for not being able to protect him and keep him safe."
— Mom

Next come the questions in your mind nonstop, lightening fast. You can't stop them: *"Why? How could this happen? Was this meant to be? How is it possible that it is meant to be? He was only thirteen, why now? Was it Karma? Whose karma, mine, his, his mother's, his brother's?"* So many questions, all with no answers. *"What could we have done to prevent this? Were we at fault? Oh my God, maybe we could have done something that would have prevented this tragedy."*

I started bike riding in earnest at the beginning of the summer, and introduced Evan to long, strenuous rides that left both of us feeling exhilarated and joyful at having completed the task we set out for ourselves. Maybe I shouldn't have done that. Maybe it's my fault.

September 3

The search for the answers to something so shocking, so unthinkable, so life altering is devastating, because when you reach for something solid to put your faith in, there is nothing but words, at least for me. Words to me are, and always have been, like menus. They can help describe things but they aren't real themselves. Words can describe a wonderful meal, but the words themselves are not the meal, no matter how much we want them to be.

I was more honest with myself. All I was left with were words, beliefs, and philosophies. I needed something real to soothe my being, some sort of cosmic salve that would heal a shattered heart and spirit. Something beyond words. For those whose faith lets them be comforted by words and beliefs, that is their personal choice. I cannot question it or relate to it.

The death of Evan immediately put our family into deep shock, which was both protecting us from the pain and numbing us to the reality that was being thrust upon us. My memories of the people coming over to our house to comfort us were that they were mainly looking after Nancy, as she was almost in a zombie-like trance. People were trying to figure out how to help her, although no one had any experience in this area. I remember Nancy's good friend Patti who came up from Pennsylvania immediately after hearing of the tragedy. She ordered Nancy to lie in the bathtub, which Nancy did for hours on end.

The memorial service and the hundreds of people that came over to our house afterwards were and still are a distant, foggy memory that we cannot seem to reconcile with the actual events. We were in a cocoon that was shielding us from the overwhelming grief that was to come in a more potent variety later on, as the deep shock wore off.

One almost impossible to comprehend task Nancy and I had to take care of was to inform all of our friends and relatives of Evan's death. That job fell to me because Nancy was in no shape to talk to anyone. I made call after call, all with such sadness and shock, on both ends of the phone. I don't understand how I could have made those calls, knowing the instantaneous horror and devastation created for those on the receiving end. It doesn't seem fair that I had the power to send so many lives reeling, leaving them powerless to overcome their feelings of grief and sadness upon hearing the news of Evan's death.

Their lives were instantly changed, and I know that those initial calls spurned a flood of other calls to friends via the telephone and Instant Messenger. The whole town of Groton and other areas of the country and the world where our family had friends felt the profound loss of Evan. It was as if a bomb had exploded and the wounded were everywhere, and in large numbers. His being gone from this world created a tidal wave of sadness and pain that washed over those who knew him and drained them of both happiness and hope. Those calls were, I hope, the hardest and most painful calls I will ever have to make, however as my shock was so total, the task actually seemed to be done by someone other than me.

September 4

Nancy and I have almost no memory of the memorial service being organized. I marvel now how well it all came together. Hundreds of

Evan's friends, family, neighbors, teachers, coaches, and people who no relationship to our family turned out to say good-bye to Evan. I know that friends of ours organized it, but I didn't know who those friends are, or how they managed to communicate the information to so many people about the funeral home viewing and the memorial service. Somehow it all worked out, and Nancy and I were being led around and told where to go and what to do. We did what we needed to, and I am so grateful to the friends who helped us at this most devastating time. We certainly could not have done it by ourselves.

People reminded us of coming to our house and talking with us after the memorial service, but Nancy and I have almost no memory of those conversations. I have almost no memory of the memorial service. I know I spoke, as did others, but it was like a dream. How could I be talking about Evan as if he were dead? He was alive in the rarest form imaginable only a few days ago. How could he be dead? He was dead. It really hadn't sunk in yet. How could it? Everything was like a horrible dream that you wanted to wake up from. I think now, upon reflection, that the conversations took place with our other selves, in the "old world." We cannot cross that gap now, as the link, at least for me, has been severed completely. They were talking to the old Mark in the old world.

Prior to the funeral service, Nancy and I went to the funeral home to spend some private time with Evan. Due to the accident and resultant death, he looked different somehow—disturbingly different, and not simply because of his injuries. His being was gone. His essence wasn't there. His body was there but Evan wasn't. It was so obvious. His hands were ice cold, and I remember how warm they felt when we first brought him home from the hospital as a baby. Now they were cold, and neither Nancy nor I could warm them up. We really wanted to.

It felt good being able to kiss him over and over and tell him how much I loved him. He wouldn't have allowed that when he was alive, the last year of his life—at least the kissing part. He would have run away screaming. Secretly, I think he liked my attempts to show affection. I miss him desperately trying to avoid my kisses. It was funny to both of us. Kisses were too un-manly when he was 13, and he was such a manly guy, but somehow his Mom's kisses were okay. It was good that he got his share before the end.

September 7

We had Evan cremated, and when we received his ashes they were in a small box, which weighed about 5 pounds, the same weight he was when he was born. Some things really do come full circle. It seems incredible that someone so big and so strong can be reduced to a small box of ashes, but that is the nature of things, the true reality. This is the fate of us all, whether we are cremated or not. We will be reduced to ashes or dust. It took us a while to get the courage to accept the ashes from the funeral home, but Nancy really wanted a part of Evan to be with her. We keep his ashes in his room in his guitar case. Nancy and I have decided to keep them rather than spreading his ashes over some beautiful place, as we had originally planned. Perhaps we will change our minds, but I doubt it. It feels like part of Evan is home with us, and that thought is quite precious and comforting.

September 8

One thing that happened almost immediately after Evan's death is that a movie began to play in my head about all the things that I did right and all the things I did wrong with Evan. It wasn't like a real movie, but there were images, thoughts and impressions about our time together. This "movie" kept playing and playing. I couldn't stop it. I can tell you honestly that my movie wasn't a horror movie, because Nancy and I tried so hard to do the right things for Evan all of his life. We made mistakes and we weren't perfect, but I can tell you that *if* that movie had more regrets about things not done and things that should have been done or could have been done, it would be the worst horror movie ever made. A personal everlasting Hell.

Hell isn't a place you go after you die with the flames and pitchforks: it's watching that movie in your head and realizing that you made so many mistakes, had so many chances to do the right thing and didn't, felt so much regret that can never be made right. Ever. Those thoughts will both torment and haunt you for the rest of your life and you will never be able to escape their grasp. It sounds pretty awful, and it is.

A formula for grief came to me. For every memory that was a pleasant one; that you were glad you did something together that was the right thing to do for your child or loved one, or provided some happiness to him/her, it's grief minus one. For every memory that was *"wish I would have, could have, should have, didn't do but could have,"* it's grief plus one. It doesn't take too much understanding to realize that you don't want to have grief plus anything, but that's not possible. Believe me, grief plus so many things undone or should have been or could have been done would be another world of pain and suffering that I cannot fathom, although I have seen it. Hopefully, the understanding you may receive by reading this book, can modify this aspect from your movie, should it play for you in the event of a loved one's death.

You never regret the things you do— only the things you *didn't* do. Of course there are always exceptions, but generally this is true, as I have sadly found out.

You begin to think that you should have taken more pictures, more videos, more of everything as you realize that there will be nothing more. Although we have literally thousands of pictures of Evan and Ryan the number seems inadequate. *"Why didn't I take more pictures, especially when he was older?"* I keep asking myself, with no answer forthcoming. One reason is that Evan didn't want to cooperate when I wanted him to "pose" for the camera when he was approaching puberty.

Two days before his death I did take some pictures of Evan on his first day of school in 8th grade. He actually stood still and posed for me. After his death, I was so out of it, I tore the roll from the camera and took it to the camera store to be developed, as I *had* to see those pictures because they were so recent. What I didn't realize is that when I had opened the camera, I exposed the film and the pictures were ruined. Pain......... *"Why was I so stupid?"* I keep asking myself. I wish I had those pictures. I wish I had those pictures almost every day. It's too late now and I have only the question. The answer doesn't matter anyhow.

The video part is especially hurtful. We have a great video camera but I didn't take as many videos of the children the last few years. *"Plenty of time,"* I thought. Now my pain is substantially increased by my lack of ambition. It's part of the process: thoughts will come to you and torment you for everything that you felt you did wrong or could have done, as you think back on the life of your child, or a friend or a loved one's life. Be prepared for the wave of horror that will accompany certain thoughts about things undone. Yet also be prepared for the happiness you will feel when you remember the good times and the things that were done the way they should have been.

Of all the video moments I wanted to capture the most precious would be Evan playing his guitar, as he was such an accomplished, amazing guitar player at such a young age. It haunted me that I didn't have any video to remember this aspect of his life. If I could have one minute to capture, it would be the sight and sounds of him wailing away on his Les Paul guitar. Nancy was going through some old videos and screamed It's *"Evan and his guitar!!!!"* I raced downstairs, and sure enough, it was a video taken on Evan's 13th birthday. I captured a sleepy Evan playing his new Les Paul, hooked up to the amplifier. Mere words cannot express my happiness. Capturing Evan playing his guitar was so important to me, and I thought I would never ever have the pleasure of seeing him play again. This was definitely one of the happiest moments of my entire life.

> *"He was the man, probably the best rock guitarist I've ever heard for a kid."*
> *— a friend*

> *"Evan you fuckin rule!!! You're the best guitarist I ever knew... and you have a sweet ass guitar... when the band gets big, we'll always remember you man!!! R.I.P. I'll never forget you."*
> *— a friend*

Another thing that really bothered us was not having Evan's voice on tape. His voice was so big and booming, and we only had his voice on tape—before it changed. When he used to hang up the phone with his mom it was funny and beautiful to hear Evan say *"I love you mommy,"* in his huge, deep voice. Evan never hung up the phone without telling her that he loved her. With me, it was typically, *"later,"* which was fine with me. I wish that everyone reading this could put their voice on tape for their loved ones, so that they can have that part of you to treasure forever, just in case.

September 17

I received a call from some of Evan's friends who had found a videotape of Evan giving a speech about how to give a speech. It was filmed in drama class while he was in 7th grade. It shows a very handsome Evan in his big voice giving a speech. I told the girls that this tape is more valuable to me than they could ever imagine, and I cannot properly express my gratitude at receiving it. It is one of the few treasures of Evan that we have showing him in his grown up form.

Why didn't I let him drive the car in a field somewhere— something he wanted to do so much," I was thinking one day. The thought came to me randomly, uninvited, and pierced my heart like a javelin being stuck through it. The mental anguish was staggering. Then I thought, *"okay, his Mom let him drive the car on the street a few times*." My pain instantly subsided. That's the way it is. Thoughts come and go and you really can't control what comes in and what stays out.

Everything now is in the past, and that is where you have to look to find pictures, art projects, music tapes, and notes that you will treasure forever. If only you think…but it's too late. Nothing else has been so permanent; everything before was fixable. *"Just give me some time"* we say, *"I'll make it right. I just need some more time. Honey, sorry, I'll make it up to you,"* we say to our spouses. *"Sorry, I didn't feel like reading with you today, let's read two chapters tomorrow,"* we say to our children. *"We'll go on that great family vacation next year, I'm too busy with work this year,"* we tell our spouses and children. *"I'll try harder in school next year. I'll work harder and fix those things that need fixing"* (in our life and our work) we tell ourselves. Now, for the first time in my life, something has happened that *cannot* be fixed with more time to do it over, to do it better, or make changes that will erase the mistakes of the past. My time with Evan has run out.

One thing is for sure; we never fully appreciate what we have until it is gone. I think we could hear this message a million times and still not understand how important it is to cherish our loved ones, our friends, and our situations until they are gone. It's human nature. This message is only at the informational stage with most people, and seemingly cannot be transferred to the knowledge stage until something drastic happens in your life, *then* we wish we had listened more or understood the message. *Then* we appreciate what we had, but it *is too late*. Life is sometimes very difficult when we cannot change things to suit our needs.

Someone recently said to me that if you had everything you have taken away and then given back to you, you would appreciate what you had. That method seems a bit on the improbable scale, but it would probably do the trick, at least for a short period of time, until we went back to taking everything for granted, once again.

If somehow, we could really get this message about appreciation, it would change the rest of our life. The process of appreciation is a lifetime mission, certainly worthy of our best efforts. I do know that, as with everything else, the effort we expend will be returned to us because we get out of things what we put into them. The effort of trying to appreciate everything we are given is a mission that we can only do our best to accomplish, and nothing more. The results will come in time, although we don't know how much time we have left on this earth, so it might not be a bad idea to increase our efforts in this area.

Appreciating what you have is possible only with the proper perspective. You may live in a place where there are lots of wild flowers, and never appreciated how beautiful they are because we take most things for granted. For someone who was just released from prison, those flowers would be magnificent—something to treasure. Our lives are filled with beauty and wonderful things, but because we are looking forward to new treasures or looking backward, we cannot live in the present, which is where all of the beauty is. Living in the moment will enhance our ability to appreciate the wonder of our lives and the gifts that have been given to us, even though we may not recognize the form the gifts take. Perhaps that is why some people call living in the moment the "present."

September 20

The loss of a child is said to be the most devastating pain a human being can experience. I agree. The anguish and the sense of loss is monumental and unparalleled in my experience. However, when a great loss happens, this is when we are being tested the most. This isn't a drill. This isn't a nightmare; *this* is a nightmare come true, and I am now faced with the question, "How do I want to spend the rest of my life?"

Will I be a victim, always feeling the numbing pain that will prevent me from living my life? Or, will I live the rest of my life to the best of my ability, in the spirit of my son Evan? I have chosen the later, as I am conscious of things that Evan would want for his family and I intend to be true to those feelings. Evan would only be proud of us if we did our best, as he did, trying to help others, regardless of the circumstances or the pain involved. Just doing your best with the cards you are dealt is all anyone can do. That is what our family is doing, in honor of Evan and in recognition of what we must do as individuals on this planet, to gain the highest and purest experience, and to gain understanding of this life.

Evan had such power and such a primal force that he was like a tuning fork that emitted a very strong and clear vibration. It is still being felt long after the tones have been struck. It is clear to me what I need to do. It's really his gift to me. It's difficult, I'm sure for someone else to understand, but I do. I really do.

September 21

After Evan's death, our family (what was left of it), went to Florida to get away for a few days. My Dad was there and it seemed like the right place to go. In retrospect it wasn't, but that's another story. We desperately needed to get away. It was too painful to be at our house; too many memories. On the plane ride to Florida I began to really struggle as to how to find the meaning to my son's life. I thought there had to be some meaning to his life and early death. There had to be, otherwise what's the point?

Then, a revelation came to me that showed me the meaning of Evan's life. A revelation is something that comes to you that doesn't involve your thought or intellectual processes. It is an understanding that you didn't have before, that doesn't involve the typical methods of gaining understanding. You don't even have to be looking for a revelation. Sometimes it just comes. You have this new understanding that can't be questioned because it is so powerful, and obviously a gift that unfogs the mirror that you may have not even known was foggy, making things incredibly clear. Your clarity is suddenly upgraded. A revelation is a gift that you don't want to refuse or not acknowledge.

When the revelation came, the part of me that was causing so much of my mental anguish fell silent. My understanding of the meaning of Evan's life on earth was a gift, given to me to share. I accept this gift. It's my obligation to share it because that's part of the gift. I literally have no choice. The question of "why" still remains and I don't think I will ever have an answer for that one, but the meaning of Evan's existence on earth is different, and understandable, with some distance from September.1st, and time to reflect on his life.

Evan had such an *extraordinary* life that I decided to write this book to tell his story, so that he won't be forgotten and to inspire others to find what they were meant to find and discover in their time on earth. Evan was an inspiration to me while he was alive, and even more so after his death. There are some people that touch you in a way that can change your life; even people in your own family. That's the way it happened to me.

This book was also cathartic, as I needed to write down my impressions of Evan and what I learned about and from him while he was alive, and after his death. Many people shared their thoughts of Evan and their experiences with him, and I started to get a clearer picture of who Evan really was. Then I knew that it wasn't entirely my story to tell. The many people that were touched by Evan and were part of his earthly adventure freely wanted to share their experiences with him because it was also cathartic for them and also helped our family to feel better about the life of our beloved son.

I have never written anything for publication prior to this book. I feel that the essence of this book is coming from a place that I don't question or understand. This isn't something I wanted to do, but something that I need to do. I also don't understand the depth of my need to write. I have never felt this way before about anything, but in this new existence there are many things I don't understand. I just try and accept them.

I don't really feel as though I am the only writer of this story. For the most part, I am just trying to stay out of the way as much as possible. There are days when I can write, and days and weeks when I haven't been able to write a word, even though I wanted to. There is a message that is trying to be delivered, and I am trying my best to be true to the way the message intends to be brought forth and to whom it is meant for. Even the title of the book was given to me— in a dream. It was so vivid and so real. I wrote the name of the title on a pad I keep beside my bed, as sometimes I'll dream about things that I want to include in the book, write them down in the middle of the night, and awaken to find that I had completely forgotten about my dream, except for the reminder on my notepad. I had already picked another title for the book and was actually arguing in my dream about it. *"This is the title for your book,"* I heard. I remembered having a dream about the title but had completely forgotten the title given to me. There on my notepad was written: Evan's Earthly Adventure.

One life can touch so many other lives in a positive way, yet be unaware of the significance of their actions. Unhappiness can be slowly turned around and happiness can be found by doing the things that you were meant to do, and doing them with all of your heart and all of your strength. A breakthrough can occur that will alter the rest of your life, but the journey isn't easy, and the ones that make it will certainly say that all of their effort was worth it. For those who don't try, they will certainly continue to make their lives pleasant, and rationalize that the prize probably wasn't worth it after all.

September 24

If there were some way to get plugged into the experience that is possible to achieve in this life, even for just a moment, there would be *huge* numbers of people longing for that experience. But, that isn't available, at least at this time. So those wanting to experience something *incredible* will simply have to search for it and keep going until they find both the meaning and experience that living life consciously will provide.

Hopefully, parents will reevaluate their parenting methods and the importance of their life with their children and their loved ones. Perhaps children will be provided with some glimmer of hope for their future, and start to question the important things in their life, similar to the method employed by Socrates, called the Socratic Method. Socrates wrote that knowledge was a living, interactive thing. Socrates' method of philosophical inquiry consisted of questioning people on the positions they asserted, and working them through questions into a contradiction, thus proving to them that their original assertion was wrong. The idea that truth needs to be pursued by modifying one's position through questioning and conflict with opposing ideas was his idea of how to arrive at the truth. Question everything! Why shouldn't we?

All of us can become life explorers, going beyond what has already been discovered by some, and making our life an exploration rather than sitting back and taking other people's thoughts and ideas and trying to make them our own, even though we truly can't. It just isn't that simple.

When you can take a close look at your own life and look within, something can open up, and during that time, when both the heart and the mind are open, something wonderful can happen. I have seen it. When people are touched enough to at least think about their life, or perhaps think about the purpose and meaning of their lives, and change something for the better, then my Evan will live on. His ability to touch people will continue, and his efforts to reach out and help others will be kept alive in the hearts of the people who are changed, even those who may never realize their connection to Evan.

> *"After going to Evan's funeral I had a better understanding of his adventurous life. Although Evan's life was cut short, he had accomplished so many things. He was so devoted to everything he did and he always did his best. By looking at the life of your son, it has helped me to look at mine. I now realize that you cannot take life for granted, it's too short. I have to put my best into everything I do like Evan did so well."*
> *— a friend*

Evan touched so many lives he never knew about, and those lives of the people that he touched will be better and richer for Evan having been alive. That is all one human being can do. Evan did what he could, to the best of his ability. There was nothing more he could have done.

> *"The years of glory Evan has brought to me are unforgettable. The times we spent together will be a part of my life for as long as I live. The memories and love that Evan has given me will always live on!! Evan had an indescribable soul. I will always love and care about Evan."*
> *— neighborhood friend*

September 25

When I think of Evan, I think my sadness is not so much about all the "what he could have been" scenarios, although those thoughts certainly exist, and continue to torture me regularly, but simply that our family misses him so very much, every day. Missing him is unbearable, in fact made worse by the knowledge that I will never see that vibrant being for the rest of my life. Ever! That thought is, and I think shall always be, haunting and a source of pain for the rest of my life.

September 26

Every day I think of Evan not being with us, and it makes me feel sad and incomplete. This isn't the way it was supposed to be. Our family is missing one person, and we didn't want him to be missing, and now he is and nothing will bring him back, and we will spend the rest of our lives missing him. Initially it was like a nightmare that only stopped when we slept, and now, it is still horrifying to think of what happened and how great our loss is. Evan was great to be with because he was so interesting; and the whirlwind that comprised his life was exciting for everyone around him. Life was always a series of *"Can you take me to the mall with my friends*?" or *"I need a ride to hockey practice. Connect me to the Internet. I need a ride to band practice,"* or *"Can I go over to so and so's house*?" It was always something, and that something was delightful to be a part of.

It was as if a bolt of pure energy was living in our house and now the energy has been transferred to another place and our house and our lives feel the loss of the energy and his presence. Our family's life now is really *boring*! WE HATE IT! We miss Evan so much, and feel that the rest of our lives will be incomplete no matter what we do or how much we accomplish. Evan is gone from this earth. It's as if a hole has been generated in my heart and the missing piece (peace) is always evident, and nothing can fill that void, no matter how much I tell myself otherwise. That isn't to say that I cannot try my best to be happy, which is my right and something that I want to do, but there is always the feeling that whatever is making me happy I would want Evan to either partake in it or share it with him. I don't think that will change, nor do I want it to. We all want to share things with those we love.

September 29

I think our family will always have a cloud over our heads, and there will never be a forecast for a completely sunny day. Maybe I'm wrong—I hope so. While many of you reading this book are perhaps contemplating what to do with the rest of your life, I am contemplating how to get through the rest of mine. There is a big difference. I will be forevermore thinking about life, death, our potential on earth and how we can achieve our goals and find real happiness. For many of you, those thoughts are almost foreign, and you have the luxury of thinking about anything you want. I don't have that luxury anymore. I don't feel I have the time to think about frivolous thoughts, as I used to. I am *very* conscious of time and I don't want to waste any of it. Not now.

October 1

After a month of staying at home after Evan's death (except for the Florida trip), Nancy, Ryan, and I finally decided that we should get out of the house. We thought perhaps it would be a good idea to go to a nearby shopping center and get our minds off of Evan and our deep sadness. Once we arrived at the shopping center it began to resemble a horror movie; everyone was acting normally, shopping for school clothes, laughing, and in general enjoying a nice Saturday afternoon at the mall. To us, it was horrifying beyond belief to be in the presence of such people. We weren't normal, we felt as though we were the walking wounded with huge visible gashes that no one could see or feel. Why were people acting so normally when Evan was dead? Why didn't they feel our pain? We rushed out of the shopping center to the safety of our home, and didn't leave it again for weeks and weeks.

When people ask how we are doing we cannot explain our feelings because there are no words to describe the emptiness and sadness we feel. Evan's death and our family's life sentence of missing him every day for the rest of our lives seems cruel and unusually harsh. Our house is eerily quiet, disturbingly so. I even miss the fighting. Nancy and I miss our Evan so much and Ryan misses his big brother more than you can imagine. Ryan says that he can't sleep alone now because Evan used to protect him because of his proximity to Ryan's bedroom. Just having Evan nearby was enough protection for Ryan to feel secure.

Nancy and I ask ourselves *"what did we do to deserve this pain*?" *"We tried so hard to be good parents, Evan turned out great. Why did this horrible thing happen? What was the point?"* The answers will never come, making the questions all the more futile, but still we ask them over and over. *"Why can't we go back to having a normal life, like we had before*," we want to know? We know we can't go back to that life, but we still ask "why." We can't help it.

October 6

"I remember Evan for the things he did accomplish and the full life he had," Evan's hockey coach, Chuck White said in a lovely letter.

Evan was able to stuff more living into his 13 years that some people who live to 100 could." If you really live your life there will be pain; it's part of living. By not striving for the brass ring, you might avoid sadness, but you certainly won't have the feeling that you reached your goal, or at least tried your best, which is still a magnificent feeling.

When I think back, I remember the good times we had: the lovely, beautiful boy who turned into a caring, kind, decent, thoughtful, talented young man. He lived his life as a halogen bulb, burning so brightly and giving off such warmth. I think he enjoyed the intensity of the concentrated light. He didn't want to be and wasn't meant to be an ordinary 75-watt bulb. He was Halogen all the way!

> *"I'm grateful now that I got the chance to see Evan when you visited last (Springtime, 2001). When I say that he was a bright, beautiful boy, I mean he gave off light, Nancy."*
> *— mother of Ryan's friend in Washington, D.C.*

If Evan had not experienced real love with his girlfriend Elizabethe, he would not have felt the pain when they had their fights. That pain is as much a part of life as was the love. It was okay for him to have the pain. He *lived* his life, and for that I am happy. Evan did achieve what all of us put on this earth can achieve, by "understanding" the clichés that make up our lives. *Always go the extra mile. Do your best. It's not whether you win or lose but how you play the game*. We hear these phrases all of our lives, and for most of us they are simply part of our collective storage repository of great things to know. It's not that we actually put those sayings into practice, but at least we have the knowledge — or perhaps we only have information — not knowledge.

The dictionary defines knowledge as wisdom or enlightenment, but how is knowledge that is not put into practice anything other than mere information? The dictionary also defines knowledge as "understanding gained by actual experience." Knowledge is knowing something as opposed to believing, which is the opposite of knowing. Information doesn't necessarily require understanding, simply inputting the facts and figures into our mind. It's the transformation from words to deeds that will define the true understanding of the words. Knowledge will only be gained by applying the information we have, which will turn into understanding. It requires action, not contemplation.

The leap from non-understanding, (the state some of us live our lives in) to a higher level of understanding is huge. It's not a small step: it's the leap that changes your life. It's the hardest leap there is. Not all of us attempt it, because we are afraid of failure or the pain associated with making the jump. Those who make it might have to try many, many times, and will suffer in the process from all the bruises from not completing the jump. There is always pain involved when we grow inwardly. There is no way around it. Although we might like to take the easy path, eventually we will discover the easy path leads nowhere, but you may not find that out until it is too late. I don't know why there is pain associated with inner growth, but I do know there is. Kahlil Gibran in his beautiful book *The Prophet* said *"Pain is the breaking of the shell that encloses your understanding."*

October 11

Evan certainly had the raw materials: good genetics, and good parenting, wonderful friends, a few excellent teachers, a marvelous hockey coach, and an awesome younger brother. The right people at the right times, sculpting and helping form the Evan he would eventually become. Evan applied the finishing touches, dedication and passion, which completed the process and formed the amazing life that Evan ended up with. Passion cannot be obtained at will, but somehow by continually applying dedication to what you are doing, the passion kicks in. Then something happens that is magical and rare and beautiful to behold; an ordinary human being that lived up to his potential. A rare sight indeed. I witnessed it in my own son.

Of course humility played a large part in the transformational process, as we cannot learn if we think we know everything. It takes the innocence of a true student to open his or her heart and mind to learn what they must. Humility is difficult to obtain, and even more difficult to maintain as we get older and our being is filled with thoughts of how much we know. It takes real courage to say that we don't know. When we open ourselves up and are willing to be taught by wise teachers, whether they are schoolteachers or not, we can reap the benefits of their knowledge and apply it to our lives, if we choose. If we are able, as Evan was, to take a look at all information and keep what we think is useful and good and disregard what we find non-useful or harmful, our lives can and will be enriched.

Evan loved to learn, about anything and everything. His appetite for knowledge was voracious and he continually tried to improve on everything he was doing or planned to do. He thought that by practicing his skills and increasing his wealth of information, he would better himself, thus creating a better future for himself, which was really important to him. Evan was quite serious about having a good future, and he knew he needed to be prepared if he was to succeed in the way he envisioned.

> *"I could tell he was a happy kid who had a bright future. The last time I saw him was Thursday afternoon (August 29,2001), pushing Kevin Harries around in a wheelchair outside of the office at Middle School. He was nice like that, always helping people. On Tuesday, when everyone went back to school, all of Evan's friends were crying and giving speeches about experiences they had with him. Everyone was so heartbroken that he had to go. It's not fair.... It really isn't. He was only 13 and he still wanted to accomplish so much more in his life."*
> *— a friend*

It wasn't until the latter part of seventh grade that Evan actually started thinking seriously about his future. Once he understood that he could achieve virtually anything he wanted, he started to think more seriously about what he wanted to do and how he needed to prepare himself. Evan really tried to get the most from his teachers, whether they were guitar teachers, schoolteachers, hockey teachers, lacrosse teachers, therapists, or anyone whom he thought he could learn from. He wasn't afraid to say *"I don't know,"* which at 13 takes a lot of courage. It takes a lot of courage at any age, if we are honest with ourselves.

"Last year Evan and I sat next to each other in math class. He amazed me with the way he always entered with a smile and worked to his highest ability. He could do anything he wanted to. Once I watched him enter the class. He walked so slowly, and so cheerfully that he just stood out from the rest of the class. While I was watching him I just began to smile and I think this shows how much he affected everyone and everything around him."
— a friend

The inspiration and dedication of this book is, of course, to my beloved son Evan, who shall remain in my heart and memory for all time. Evan started something by living life the way he did. It's the least Nancy and I can do: to fan that spark that his hard work and passion for living started, and help turn the spark into a fire that will have sufficient warmth and light to act as a beacon in the search and struggle for truth. Sounds dramatic, but the reality is that people do need beacons, and those beacons are the people who by their actions, not words, blazed a trail that others want to follow because they know where the trail will lead.

Too many people don't know which trail to follow because the numbers of people who seem truly happy doing what they are doing are so few. We don't have many beacons to turn to in times of hopelessness and despair, and that is certainly when we most need the warmth of the fire that Evan's spark created. The fire is available for everyone, but only those who are seeking and open will be able to partake in its warmth. That's just the way it works. We certainly have enough negative images available to us. Those images and the people who represent those images are very attractive to the younger generation: shocking images and shocking people have always held an attraction for every youthful generation.

By contrast, the opposite images that counterbalanced the "scary" people, which are typically the rock stars, are so squeaky clean and wholesome that there is a large group of teenagers that don't have any image to turn to and say "that's the kind of person I would like to emulate." There doesn't seem to be any middle ground.

Evan

I can't put down precise dates on this section as I am simply remembering him.

Evan knew he had the power. He just started feeling it this past year (2001), and slowly began to put it to use. Experimenting at first, and then putting it into operation in more situations, feeling empowered even more by the results. Something wonderful was happening right in our midst; and it was being witnessed by his family, his friends, his teachers, and his coaches. We were all witnessing real understanding and the resultant effects of the dual combination of effort and passion on one beautiful human boy. It was a sight I have never seen before, at least in person.

A friend who had read a rough draft of this book talked to me about raising his children. His own old 13 year old son isn't as motivated as Evan, and isn't putting the best he has into everything the way Evan did. His son hadn't yet found himself like Evan. *"How did Evan do what he did*?" It's a good question, and I don't actually have the answer. Only by doing what Evan did will you find out what he experienced. You cannot simulate effort and produce a simulated passion. As they say, *"life isn't a spectator sport*," although many of us live our whole lives as spectators, rooting for the players who are having all the real fun and the excitement of being alive. Their lives are a series of adventures, rather than a burden or something to get through.

It's also not fair to compare children to Evan, since he was a very rare individual and we cannot be like him. No one can be exactly like another person; we shouldn't even want to be. We should care about being the best "us," not a lesser version of someone else. That's all we can do. We won't understand what Evan felt until we give life our best shot. Then maybe, we can become the person we were meant to be.

I think some of us have experienced short glimpses of "going for it" in our lives, and we've seen others do it, but the duration was inevitably short lived. The results were less than we anticipated. Perhaps that is why we gave up before reaching our goals. Also, the path is hard and some of us want instant results, so we try taking the easier path, hoping to end up in the same place. I don't think there is an easier path, but if there were, the feeling when you reached the end would certainly not be as glorious as taking the harder route and succeeding. Is it better to fail taking the harder path, or succeed taking the easier path? It's an interesting question. Perhaps you could succeed on the harder path, but how would you know, if you took the easier way?

> *"Evan was one of the most unique friends I had. He was almost perfect in my mind. Whenever he was around, in a group or by himself, he would always bring a smile with him. Always upbeat, he gave me the impression of comfort and joy when he was around. He wasn't afraid to try anything. Great at sports, music, school, social situations, and the list goes on. He had his whole life ahead of him, with so many goals as well. He always turned something that was bad into something that was good."*
> *— a friend*

Evan had short-term and long-term goals, which he started formulating in the fifth grade. They became more realistic when Evan turned into a teenager. He kept working toward his goals and putting in more and more effort, and he didn't stop, even when it got really, really hard. In fact, that's when he worked even faster. Somewhere along the way he found the passion. Evan was able to reach his goals and felt the power that only one who has attained something through sheer will and effort can understand. I noticed that Evan was happier than he had been previously. I don't think it was a coincidence, although, just like the rest of us, there were still periods when things weren't great, but he continued to move forward, regardless of what life was throwing at him.

> *"Being one of Evan's Hockey Coaches last year and this year has been a great privilege. It was his passion for not only Hockey but everything he did which I will remember. Everything, whether it was hockey, lacrosse, doing sit-ups, pushups, lifting weights, or even riding his bike was done with passion.*
> *So all of his classmates, teammates, and friends, whether you are doing a school assignment, playing in a hockey or lacrosse game, think of Evan and do it the way he did it, do it with passion.*

And no matter what any scoreboard says, if you have done it the way Evan would have you are truly a winner."
— Chuck White, Evan's hockey coach, shared these thoughts at Evan's memorial service.

We all can accomplish more than we think we can. Although, for most of us, we don't have specific goals that we set for ourselves, and we aren't prepared to do everything possible to obtain those goals. Then we wonder why we aren't as happy as we would like to be and wonder why our life hasn't turned out the way we envisioned. Life can still be good, but is it the best we can make it? Or have we settled for pretty good, or just okay? Have we searched for true happiness, which I think some of us realize can only be achieved by connecting to the spiritual aspect of our lives, not material things, good jobs or relationships? If so, perhaps you understand the importance of this connection. If not, then perhaps it is something to explore.

There is that old saying that some of us may be able to relate to, *"be careful of what you wish for, you just might get it."* How many of you have had your dreams fulfilled at one point in your lives, and don't feel fulfilled? How much are you willing to put into your life to make it wonderful? How many changes do you have to make? How many sacrifices do you need to make? How much do your goals mean to you? Anything less than all you have will produce results that are less than you want.

Evan Holofcener at the age of thirteen was simply *awesome.* In his short time on earth, he managed to cram in lifetimes of passion, dedication, inspiration, courage, and kindness. His dear friend and neighbor Amanda dropped off a note for us, which contained this quote from Abraham Lincoln:

"A*nd in the end it's not the years in your life that count it's the life in your years. I think this quote in some ways says it all,*" Amanda noted.

And to his family, his friends, his teammates, his teachers, and even those who knew him casually, we were all aware that a special person was in our midst and we enjoyed his presence and benefited so much from it. We will all remember Evan for the remainder of our days. For when a human is born with such potential, and lives up to that potential, that one single act of determination can change things. It has already started. The letters that are quoted in this book are a testament to the effect Evan had on people. I didn't think it would be right to talk about how my son touched others, other than to say that he did. That is best left up to those people whose lives he touched.

Interestingly enough, Evan never realized how many people he touched. In fact he talked often about how no one would miss him when he was gone. That seemed unusual as he was only thirteen at the time. He didn't understand how simple acts of kindness that he showed to his friends were so appreciated. He also wasn't fully aware of how his peers viewed him. Evan was someone rare and special, and his friends both knew this and appreciated his uniqueness. He was however, focused on doing what he both wanted to do and what he needed to do. He understood that he had the ability to do things better than just about everyone, but he didn't get a swelled head about it.

Evan is missed by so many people. I only wish he could see all of the cards, letters, emails and the dedications and testaments to him. I think he would be really happy and really surprised.

> *"Although I didn't know Evan very well I'm still sad that he's gone because I see all the people that were close to Evan crying, those people make me even more sad than I already am. He was a special person because I realize that for one person to have such a giant impact on such a large group of people is amazing."*
> *— a schoolmate*

> *"Evan and I were pretty close friends. Last year we were on the same team in school. I often found myself having conversations with Evan at lunch or on the phone. He was one of the happiest, funniest, most determined kids I'd ever met. I miss him more than imaginable. It's still hard for me to believe that he is gone. It feels like I am empty inside.*
> *I feel sorry for every person who didn't know Evan because talking to him for 30 minutes was better than talking to some*

people for hours on end because he was so full of insight. If you ever had a problem, whether it was big or small, Evan would take the time to sit down with you until you worked things out. He always gave the best advice and all his words had strong meaning behind them. Anything he talked about (which was usually guitar) was filled with so much passion. He truly loved everything that was going on in his life, and that's not something you usually find in teenagers. He is probably the best person I will ever meet and I am proud to call him one of my closest friends."
— a friend

This poem was received by a fellow poet and classmate:

"I never knew you
And now you're gone
I'll never get that chance
I almost knew you,
That smoldering day
Stuffed into the lacrosse pads
But I didn't
I screwed up
Now I never will
Or maybe, just maybe I can, I will
Maybe by looking into your friends
Analyzing those who weren't
Like me I never was
I missed out
Now I ache for what I never had"

We have so many letters and emails from friends saying how much he was loved, but most of those letters also mentioned that they never told Evan of their love for him. Now they are doing so, which is good, but it would have been better, for them and for Evan, if those kids had been able to find the courage and the time to tell him how they felt while he was alive. Although it is understandable that teenagers are not accustomed to speaking from their heart and letting people know how much they mean to them. That may be "uncool," and coolness is something that prevents us from doing some of the things we want to do. It also keeps us from doing what we need to do, and that's sad.

> *"Never forget me Evan, because I will always have you in my heart. I love you! I've never said that to anyone before but I'm glad you're the first."*
> *— excerpt from a letter sent after Evan's death*

Evan was always protective of his friends and would do whatever he could to help, still never knowing how much those small acts he performed meant to those that he helped.

> *"Evan I will never forget you! I remember once I was in the mall and this kid was being mean to me so you walked up to someone you didn't know and said 'say your sorry, say it like you mean it.' That was the nicest thing anyone has ever done for me. Evan you are soo awesome."*
> *— a friend*

The most interesting thing about this encounter at the mall was that Evan never mentioned it to his mom or me. I think I would have been bursting to tell my parents about my manly adventure, but that's me—not Evan.

> *"One of my favorite memories would have to be when I saw him once at the mall. I was with my friend and a group of guys kept following us around. We wanted them to stop, so we found Evan and <u>he</u> followed them around the mall. They got so scared of him and he thought that was just the coolest thing ever. Once we caught up with the frightened kids, all we could do was laugh at them! We all had the best time that day."*
> *— a friend*

There were many other stories similar to this one sent by Evan's friends, but I think you get the point that Evan was there for his friends, and would protect and defended them at all times.

A poem written by one of Evan's friends:

"I took you for granted
And now I can't apologize.
You were an awesome friend and one of the best people I will ever know.
Everything came easily to you,
Whether it be guitar, or lacrosse, you were amazing.
Now that you're gone,
It feels like my body is an empty shell.
An eerie cold always surrounds me,
No heat can help it, for it comes from the inside.
I find myself staring into space,
I'm not sure whether it's because I have too many thoughts flowing through my mind
Or if it's because I'm using all the power that I can find inside of me to try and get you back.
I don't know how much of my life is based on reality anymore.
Sometime I see someone, thinking it's you,
Or I find myself searching for you in the morning; my mind still believes this is all a joke.
I ask God how come it was you,
Why couldn't it have been me?
So young with so many opportunities waiting ahead.
I will that you will go far wherever you are
And will complete whatever is planned for you in heaven.
You're a **star***, watching over the world watching over me.*
When anything is accomplished by me,
It will be done only because a part of your spirit is in my heart;
Hundreds of times I've wanted to give up on life,
To come and see you again, but then, maybe without knowing it, you put some sensible
Thoughts in my mind; you give me the strength to live.
I love you more than imaginable.
Evan though you are gone, you will live in my heart and soul.
I cannot wait until the day we meet again.
Godspeed and good luck."

Background

It wasn't always easy for Evan. He was born to a loving, nurturing mother who cherished Evan from the moment he was born. Nancy is beautiful, smart, kind, cool, compassionate, passionate about life and learning, artistic, and a wonderful wife and mother. Evan was so much a part of her. It was as if Nancy created a wild and wonderful sprig from her being. Nancy respects all living things, including the earth itself. She works hard to make everything better than she found it. Her efforts are the labors of love, making our home and our family her workshop. She was and is always trying to provide the love and nurturing necessary for optimum growth. Of course I loved Evan from the moment he was born as I did Ryan, but I was scared at the reality of being a new dad. Nancy, on the other hand seemed to know what to do right away.

Nancy creates beautiful gardens wherever she is, to give her the pleasure of being in nature, and she loves the simplicity of planting seeds and watching them grow into beautiful creations. Evan was like the garden: A seed was planted, and with the proper love, training, nurturing, weeding, the right ingredients, and not being afraid to let the garden grow wild sometimes, it grew into something wonderful.

Evan was always surrounded by animals. He was so small (5 lbs.) at birth, that when he was brought home from the hospital he was placed in a sleeping basket on our bed, with soft blankets to support him. At that time, we had three cats and all of the cats arranged themselves in a circle around the basket whenever Evan was sleeping. It was an interesting and beautiful site to behold.

Evan was part of nature, as we all are. It was because of his love of nature and animals that Evan, from the day he was born to the day he died, was a true vegetarian. He never once ate meat, fish or chicken, or *"anything with a face,"* as we like to say. He had too much respect for the animals. That was his choice, as it has been ours; we gave him the choice of not becoming a vegetarian, but to him that was unthinkable. We always told him he was free to try meat at his friend's houses, but he would always say *"that's gross."* We agreed.

Before Evan was born, his mom (in her typical fashion), got all the books on how to raise a baby and take care of him the in best way possible. That's her way: to educate herself on how to do the best job, and then do it. The books all seemed to have good advice, although sometimes the advice was conflicting. It's an interesting phenomenon when you have conflicting advice on how to sleep train the baby, for example. How are you supposed to know which expert to believe? Certainly you could always try the trial and error approach, as we did. One way worked, the other didn't. The way that didn't work was painful for all of us.

Was it just a matter of believing one bit of advice over another? If so, is that how life is supposed to be—a random selection of thoughts and advice that appeals to you? Do we reject the information we don't like or agree with prior to knowing more about it, and keep the information that seems sensible (according to our upbringing) or fashionable? How can we know what we don't know?

Nancy took parenting classes from PEP (Parent Encouragement Program) a parenting organization located in the Washington, D.C. area. She wanted to better her understanding of how to best raise our children in the manner that we felt was more consistent with the way we wanted our children to grow up—empowered and free of the typical parenting actions that are so dominant in this society. Nancy first began taking classes at PEP which were based on the principles of Alfred Adler, and then began teaching them. Teaching kept us close to a group of people who were really trying hard to raise conscious children.

We exposed Evan to Judaism, Christianity, Buddhism, and other spiritual ideas and told him to find his own truth. We never raised him in any particular religion and we never gave him a set of beliefs and said *"okay, here is what you believe in."* We truly felt that burdening him with a pre-conceived concept of religion would not be beneficial for him. Evan had the mindset of an explorer and would find his own way, which Nancy and I have, by searching and comparing various religious and spiritual paths. Why would we raise Evan in a different manner? It made him feel excited that he could be a spiritual adventurer.

It's interesting to note that we as parents give our children so many ideas about life, but eventually they choose their own path. Typically they don't follow our line of work, or like the same music, or dress the way we do, or appreciate the same things we do, but interestingly enough many still cling to the same religion we do. It's a curious phenomenon. Perhaps our children have never really thought about their religious beliefs, so therefore don't elect to choose their own path as they have with everything else.

Nancy and I talked to Evan about everything but it was mostly Nancy whom he talked to as he got older. It made Evan feel, rightly so, that we cared about him. Nancy patiently waited for the right time for him to open up and share his thoughts, hopes, dreams, cares, problems, and just ordinary stuff. Once he started talking, (usually at bedtime), it was hard for him to stop. Nancy gave him the time he needed to unload, and he loved that. It was important for us to talk to Evan about the important things in life, spirituality, hope, fears, the future, God, and always music. Oftentimes, I felt as though he wasn't listening, but he was.

> *"He had so much compassion for others and I thought he was such a deep person. I was so impressed by him. A few weeks ago he was on Instant Messenger trying to cheer up and guide a fellow classmate in his time of need. I was so impressed, and I really enjoyed talking to him myself.*
> *Some people just touch you in a special way. While Evan was 'a kid', who did the things kids will do as they seek to understand this world, I was impressed by his ability to express himself, and his open-mindedness. He was a boy, it seems to me, way beyond his years spiritually. He had a beautiful spirit; brighter than any I've seen in a person his age. I was so looking forward to watching him grow up.*
>
> *I really felt that Evan had a lot to offer my kids in a "spiritual" way. I just saw so much innocent love in him. He wasn't perfect-he was human, but he had a good heart and was on a good path. I thought he was a rare kind of person, the kind I wanted in my kid's lives. The kind you can talk to and know he*

will speak honestly with you. He was a person whom I felt was going to make a real difference in people's lives. He did make a difference. Everyone was so happy when he was around. We all will miss him so much, and his bright spirit will continue to make a difference in the lives of those who knew and loved him, like us."

— note from a neighborhood mom

We talked to Evan quite a bit about spirituality and how important it is to have it in your life if you ever expect to be happy. He rejected much of what we said as is typical of most kids getting advice from their parents, but I think he finally understood that aspect of life, and was delving into it in his own way. Happiness is inside of you, not outside. I mean literally, not figuratively. It's simply not just a catchy phrase, but something that can be defined as real in the way you would describe anything as real (as compared to a belief or philosophy). Something real can be experienced via our five senses. That is how we can know if something is real or not.

"When did you lose that which has always been within you? When did you lose that which resides within you? When did you lose that very thing that keeps you alive? When did you lose that one thing within you that is the source of all of your aspirations? When did you lose that thing that is the source of all your joy? When did you lose that thing that is the source of all peace in your life?

I have to say that I never lost it, and I don't know of a single human being on the face of the Earth that has lost it, because it resides within you. Maybe I have lost contact with it-I can understand that. And if so, I need to reestablish that contact. I need to hear "me" once again. You realize what that implies? Once again, I need in the silence within to re-address myself-my life, my priorities, my relationship with myself-and to enjoy being in the company of that one most beautiful thing that there is."

— Maharaji, June 16, 1997

We gave Evan the best gifts that parents can give to their children: faith, trust, hope, humor, the lessons about all people being equal, and the assurance he was truly loved. He knew this from the bottom of his heart. He felt loved and took solace in the unwavering love of his family. It helped Evan when times were tough to know that we loved him no matter what. I really think he used this resource on a number of occasions, even though he would have denied it.

> *"I want to thank you so much for the way you brought Evan up. You can tell in one conversation that he was raised to love, to believe in what he feels, and to respect. Evan was a "perfect kid," he was full of happiness and so much love."*
> *— a friend*

Nancy and I didn't hold back the things he needed to hear and we needed to say. We weren't afraid to hug and kiss him for no reason. Of course, as he got older this became more of a problem. He thrived on our allowing him to explore and question. Evan was blessed with a natural curiosity that basically involved everything. He wanted to know how things worked and how things reacted when placed together, and wouldn't dismiss anything out of hand without first trying to understand it and learn about it for himself.

We brought Evan up to question authority, even mine. I told him not to swallow all the stuff that people were saying. Well meaning stuff, most of it, however he needed and was given permission to find his own way. He loved that. Once in a while I forgot that I told him to challenge me, and this created some problems, but I am glad his mom and I gave permission to Evan to challenge everything and to find his own understanding. Looking back now, I wouldn't have changed a thing.

November 2

I talked with our wonderful family therapist, Dr. Amy Lew, about Evan and the power struggle that occurred for a period of time between us. Evan and I talked to Dr. Lew about our problems, together and individually. In our family we have a very high opinion of counseling, and we have been fortunate to find some very good counselors; in times of stress and trouble, we weren't afraid to get help.

"Evan," Dr. Lew commented, *"showed a lot of courage taking you on."* In her opinion, he was trying to help me become the dad that he knew I could be. I thought about that and realized that she was right, although I would never have come to that conclusion myself in a million years. That shows you the value of perspective. This "taking me on" was a loving fight although it didn't feel that way sometimes. Evan was trying to help me, but I didn't realize it at the time. I felt that Evan won our power struggle and showed that he was the better man, and I am not ashamed to admit it.

Theoretically no one wins a power struggle, but I felt as though it came at a time in our lives when it needed to happen for both of us. Evan was taking on the dominant male (me) and trying to establish his own identity within the family structure. He did. I acted in a manner that showed my lack of understanding about a lot of things at that time, and I wish that I could have another chance to do things differently, but that is not to be. I have to live with the knowledge that I was being helped by Evan to find the better me, the me that I should have been all along. The me that I thought existed, but wasn't sure would ever surface.

November 5

In the fall of 1997 our family moved from Washington, D.C. (where we lived most of our lives) to Groton, Massachusetts where I had a good job opportunity. Washington, D.C. was becoming a difficult place to live; the school system was awful and the ever-increasing crime was starting to affect the way we lived our lives. Groton was paradise for Evan. He blossomed in the rural atmosphere, with its beautiful scenery, wholesome kids, and an abundance of nature always surrounding him. The crime rate was almost nonexistent, and Evan felt safe in this small community. That wasn't the case in Washington, D.C. He enjoyed the freedom of being able to ride his bike around town, going "uptown" with friends, and walking around the block at night with no supervision. Simple pastimes did indeed bring him so much pleasure. He told friends this past summer that to him *"Groton was paradise."* I really think we moved to Groton just for Evan.

Groton was safe, or so we thought. A typical small New England town, there isn't even a traffic light, and there are no parking meters on the main street, which is simply called Main Street. Since the area is so picturesque, there are many bike riders riding in and through Groton. The drivers in the area are used to the bikers and tended to give them wide berth when sharing the road. It all seemed so safe.

> *"Evan thought that Groton was paradise. He never thought that paradise would kill him. He also loved his bike and who would have thought that he would have died on something that he loved. This great kid had his whole wonderful life ahead of him and it was shortened by his love to ride."*
> *— a friend*

When Evan arrived in Groton he was in the fourth grade. He was so scared about going to a new school and meeting new people that he had a mild panic attack the day before school started. He was really concerned about fitting in and people liking him. Here he was this handsome, smart, nice kid and he wasn't really secure in himself. From looking at him you would think he would be, but he wasn't. He lacked self confidence and we could never figure out why.

Evan was also concerned that everyone in Massachusetts spoke like the Kennedys, and that *"pahk the cahr in Havad yahd"* would be the way children spoke. We told him this wasn't the case, but I'm not sure he totally bought it. He didn't want to be so different: he just wanted to fit in. This attitude would change dramatically in time. Fortunately, there were only a few kids who spoke like the Kennedys. Evan wrote on his first day of school in Groton *"I remember my first day of school in Mrs. Antonelli's class. Everybody was so nice: I was trying to figure out who was faking it because it was my first day. I found out nobody was."* I thought it was interesting that Evan was on the lookout for people faking sincerity when he was nine years old.

At Florence Roche Elementary school he auditioned for the play, *Sleeping Beauty*, so that he could make new friends. In Groton, the school plays are not your typical fourth grade play. They were incredible productions with amazing choreography and music, complete with artistic backdrops and a large chorus. Evan was awarded the role of Prince Charming, the male lead. He was simply beautiful, and when he transformed from the Blue Faun into the Prince, the audience was stunned at both the transformation and the actual regal presence Evan exuded.

> *"Evan was one of the sweetest kids I ever knew. I met him first during the Sleeping Beauty play. I called him my "Little Faun." Ms. Jeffrey (play director) put me in charge of keeping Evan still (he always had a lot of energy, sometimes a little too much). We kept in touch throughout our years in middle school together, but I sometimes regret never telling him that I loved him. Well Evan, I love you."*
> *— a friend*

November 6

In fifth grade, Evan wrote in a year end summary: *"This year of school was the best year I've ever had. I will never forget this year for two reasons. This was the year I got in trouble the most but learned the most. I learned that you should always go the extra mile because it pays off. Like on my reports I got two A+s and two A-s. Of course I learned a lot of math but the lessons I learned about trying hard and doing the best you can were more important to me."*

I found this summary after Evan's death when we were going through some of his papers. Nancy and I never realized at that time how important the idea of doing the best you could meant to him. We say so many things to our kids, but most of us never know if any of it is really getting through.

Evan was morphing both physically as well as in his ability to understand the true meaning of the phrases that people keep repeating; *"Always go the extra mile, it will pay off, Great Job!"* Mr. Knepifer,

Evan's teacher, wrote on Evan's 5th grade report about Sir Francis Drake. At the time Evan read the comment and thought it was nice, and was especially proud of the A+ he received. It wasn't until two years later that he really understood the meaning of those words and started to put them into action. It was then that his life changed.

This past summer right before Evan was to prepare for his 8th grade classes, he took Mr. Kneipfer's comment on the Sir Francis Drake report and placed it in his collection of special things, and told us that he would keep that report forever. The words were being understood and absorbed, from mere ink to a way of life. A richer, fuller life. When I contacted Mr. Kneipfer and told him what Evan had said about his feelings toward him and the battle cry that became so real for Evan Always go the extra mile it will pay off, Mr. Kneipfer told me that it was his proudest moment as a teacher. His going the extra mile with Evan paid off for him, too. That's the way it should be.

> *"Evan liked to do just about anything. His personality was one of a kind in that he never worried what others might think. He loved sports, but he also seemed to dabble and enjoy other less cool experiences like poetry and acting.*
>
> *When we used to play basketball together as a class I naturally laid off quite a bit so as not to accidentally hurt anyone. I remember one day, however, Evan was playing and knocked into me trying to grab a loose ball. Usually 5th graders bounce right off me, but he was so big and strong he nearly took me out! My knees buckled, I went flying and barely managed to keep my balance! I turned around and looked at him with a "holy cow" After that, I played a lot harder when he had the ball and I believe I told him so. He still scored on me way too much for my own liking and I remember thinking "this kid's gonna mop the floor with me in a few years and he's only 10.*
>
> *Evan was the true leader of that 5th grade class. Everyone liked him. All the boys copied the things he would do. And most of the girls had crushes on him at one time or another. Ms. Guernsey often commented how strikingly good-looking he was for a boy*

> *that age (our nickname we called him amongst ourselves was Brad Pitt).*
>
> *There would always be a trail of wanna-be's following him everywhere he would go. I think he liked the attention to a point, but I always knew he wasn't entirely comfortable with it; it added pressure to his life that he really didn't want. I wish the other kids would leave him alone more. I would say "Evan's not a superkid, he's just like the rest of you only taller and blonder. Try and be yourself and not him." They would nod their heads and agree, but a day later there would be a gang of them sitting around Evan hanging on his every word."*
>
> *— comments from Mr. Kneipfer in a letter to Nancy and me after Evan's death*

This pattern would continue to follow Evan throughout his life. It was interesting to observe the reaction of Mr. Kneipfer when I told him how much he had meant to Evan and to our family; how much he influenced and brought out the best in Evan at precisely the right time. Mr. Kneipfer was shocked to find out how much impact he actually had on Evan, and said that he felt scared knowing how much he could affect his students, for the better or for the worse. He said that he would now pay more attention to how he interacted with his students. I felt that his scared feeling was good because it was consciousness surfacing that enabled him to *see* how he could have more influence on the students he was teaching.

When he asked me if there was anything he could do, I told him to share the feelings he was having with other teachers, and he said he would. My heart felt slightly better that night. I am and will always be thankful to Mr. Kneipfer for his relationship with Evan.

Evan was always on the cutting edge. He had so many kids looking to him for leadership in how to be cool and for having the answers that I think it pushed Evan harder than he would have normally pushed himself. It also added great pressure on him that was unusual for someone his age. He was never able to let his guard down, except when he at was home or at rock concerts. I felt sorry for him too at times, as did his mom.

> *"I have so many questions that don't have any answers. I wish you were here to help me. Is it really worth living, I know the answer is YES but there is so much pain inside me. I wish it was me instead of you! You had so much going for you and you were friends with everyone. You were a hero for everyone that knew you and everyone that didn't know you. Everyone looked up to you. Will I ever see you again? Will I ever be able to talk to you again? If you are gone, can you talk to who ever you want? What makes me so sad is that I will never see you again. Where are you when I need you ? Whenever I was sad you would say something and make it all better."*
> *— a friend*

> *"Evan was truly a star, in every way. He did everything to a level of perfection. It hurts everyday not seeing him at school."*
> *— a friend*

Since Evan left this world at his peak, he has become somewhat larger than life. Stories about him, as I have seen personally, are growing by leaps and bounds. His image and place in the hearts and minds of his peers will be set forever. Evan will always remain thirteen, handsome, daring, adventurous, full of energy, full of wisdom, full of life, and passion. The memory will never fade or become dull or diminished by time. Evan will forevermore be Evan at his best to all of us who knew him.

> *"Evan and I were always talking in the 5th grade play, "The Emperor's New Clothes." He was a lord and I was a lady of the court. We couldn't help smiling at each other while we were acting our parts. Evan and I would always be laughing, talking, joking, and having fun. He was the kind of person that made being in the play all that much more fun and exciting. I had a great time that year."*
> *— a friend*

Things were beginning to stir within Evan. An awakening seemed to be taking place inside of him. He was starting to figure things out in ways that were both clear and magical to him. If you just do an average job, you will grow up to become an average person, and that is the last thing Evan wanted to be! But how do you get to be more than average? He was just starting to understand the way to go beyond average. Effort certainly was a primary ingredient, but something later on would change the mixture of his life dramatically. This new ingredient would propel him to a higher level of existence.

November 11

In sixth grade, Evan described himself on the first day of school in a letter to his new teacher.

"I am a very big learner. For instance, I am learning how to play the guitar and more school related I am finding out how important it is to be organized. I am also trying to put together a band.

"For a whole person I am just a happy go lucky guy. I think I am kind of funny and I like to have fun, but I am also very athletic and active. For the more physical stuff I am 5'3" and have hazel eyes and blond hair. I always feel more comfortable being around people but some times I just want to reflect on my feelings and just plain old think."

In the sixth grade, Evan became more of the Evan that he would eventually become. A sharp sense of humor accompanied this change.

> *"I remember when I first met Evan. In sixth grade guidance class, the teacher paired us off. In each group, we had to learn something about each other. I was paired with Evan. We were asking each other questions, and Evan took staples and put them all the way up his ears, lips, nose and eye brows. It looked like he had a massive amount of piercing. At the time I was kind of put off, but now I understand that he was really being funny. Evan was a great person and I will never forget that."*
> *– a schoolmate*

"When I first moved to Groton in 1999 the first friend I had was Evan. "He volunteered to show me around school. He sat with me at lunch and showed me what to do and not to do. He told me what each teacher was like, if they were mean or not. We hung out together and talked a lot. He was really involved with music. He was in chorus until Ms. Kennaugh kicked him out for talking. Evan liked to talk, he was very social. He was a true friend and I will always miss him."
— a friend

November 12

In seventh grade, things were not going well with regard to Evan's schoolwork. His natural intelligence simply wasn't enough to get him on the Honor Roll which he had easily achieved every year, without much studying. It sort of devastated him, knowing that he had simply run out of his "built in" smarts. It was the first time that he had to put effort into his schoolwork. If he didn't, he knew he would be like so many kids, getting sort of good grades, but that wasn't sufficient for Evan. Yet, he didn't seem to be interested in working that hard because his social life was definitely taking on more importance, and Nancy and I felt that we needed to give him the space to be able to enjoy this social aspect of school. Evan was delighted to be able to spend so much time on Instant Messenger, talking to his friends for hours and hours at a time.

Nancy once found Evan downstairs at his computer at 2:00 a.m. talking to some friends online. We thought that was a bit much, but we were happy that Evan was part of a vast social scene. We felt good for him that he was so popular, and having more friends seemed to make him happier. Another time, Nancy found him up again at around 2:00 a.m.; this time he was watching a video Nancy had given him on the value of getting enough sleep!

November 18

Trouble started brewing earlier in the school year. Evan had a difficult time in the first few months of seventh grade. His skin was breaking out, and his voice changed from that of a boy to a deep-throated man. One of the first times I called our house when his voice had changed and heard this deep voice say *"Hello."* I immediately hung up the phone thinking that I had dialed the wrong number. Nope. That was my new Evan. I had to notice that he was morphing into a man.

Evan wore black clothes to school every day during those first few months, and came home with drawings on his hands and arms; symbols: that he got out of his guitar magazines. It was actually quite scary. We were worried about him. He was sort of worried about himself. Puberty had begun in earnest and the hormones were confusing to him. He was going through a huge growth spurt and was trying so hard to figure out who he was and where he belonged, in school and in life. He also wanted to make a statement that he wasn't like anyone else. What was he? Was he a kid who only wore black clothes and could only sit at the lunch table of the other kids who wore only black clothes? Did he want to be like everyone else who seemed to be happy and were dressed like models out of Abercrombie & Fitch? His poetry during that time was filled with references to the fact that he wore a mask to school every day that hid the pain; as did so many others, even those happy acting preppies.

Written by Evan during this period:

> *I look out from my pit of pain and misery. My hands stained with hate and anger. To see you, a hope and a dream walking, looking down on me. You put out your hand to lift me out of the hole I have so willingly dug and emerge into a new world. A world where everyone wears a mask. A mask made of insecurity and doubt. A doubt that they won't fit in, a doubt that they won't be accepted. You all smile but it's all a lie. A lie! I can't live in this fake world, but I must. I must arise every morning and put on my mask to lie to the world to tell them I am OK. If only they knew... If only.*

Interesting enough, other people felt differently about Evan and were able to see behind the mask, although I don't think that Evan believed anyone would be able to. He felt very alone.

A good friend and fellow poet wrote this poem to him after his death.

Forever
You always thought that you were alone
And that your pain would remain unknown
It was a pain you thought no one could see
A familiar pain, because it lives inside me
You always thought no one would care
If they woke one morning, and you were no longer there
But now you see that you were wrong
And your spirit will live, long after you're gone
Something we will always remember
Is that bitter day in Early September
We always knew this day would come
But when it did, we all went numb
In a flash, your life was taken
But you will never be forsaken
Where you left this world, flowers lay
And in our hearts you will forever stay

Evan's art and poetry was really flourishing during this period, but interestingly enough Evan only wrote poetry when he was unhappy. I have only once seen a poem written about anything happy, or written when he was in a good mood. His art tended to be figures that were dark and gloomy, like the "Nightmare before Christmas" figures that he was always drawing. That's just the way he was….. at this time in his life.

This poem was written by Evan to Elizabethe

I'll never forget you
The way you'd tell me you love me
How you never gave up on me
The way you held me
The way your hands feel

How you always made me smile
Your soft eyes
How you made me feel like I wasn't worthless
I love you
More than you can ever imagine
I know it's not healthy
But I don't care,
They say love will go on forever
Is this love?
Will we last forever?
Or will you give up on me?
They say that once you are depressed
And you get better
You will never be normal again
That you will never be completely happy
I wish I could forget everything
I'm still haunted by my thoughts
I am still scared
I can't forget
My arms, a constant reminder of what I was
My hands still stained
My mind, still scared
I wish
That I could forget it all
All the pain
Sometimes it's too much
And I give in
To the thoughts that still haunt me
I'm worthless"
Sometimes, I hate myself
And I wish I didn't exist
Wishing I was gone
Forgotten
My memories tear at the walls of my sanity
Memories are all I have left
Memories and dreams
Dreams that you won't leave me

Hoping you will still love me
wish I could go back

It was a tough time for Evan and for our family. Lots of counseling, both family counseling and individual counseling for Evan. Evan felt really good when coming out of the therapist's office. Of course he told his friends he didn't tell the therapist anything, but as we found out after his death, he was quite revealing. We understood that the therapist would only tell us the content of their sessions if he felt that Evan was under any threat of hurting himself. Our hope was that Evan could talk to someone if he felt he couldn't talk with us, which was in fact the case. Evan needed someone to talk to and help him sort out the issues he was dealing with. Kids his age would be of no use in helping Evan because he was typically dealing with issues that wouldn't be presented to them for quite some time.

However, romance was certainly a part of his life, and it made him incredibly happy and incredibly sad, depending on which week it was.

Written by Evan

I put my arm around her and slowly caressed her arm with my fingers. Her skin was soft and warm and she smelled lightly of Tommy Girl. She curled up towards me and put her hand on my arm and her head on my shoulder. I looked at her, she is so beautiful. I stared into her eyes and loved her even more. She is perfect. I whispered 'I love you,' gently into her ear, she looked at me and learned forward, my lips met her in a sweet embrace. It was perfect. Nothing was as perfect as us. She pulled away. "I love you" she whispered to me. She is perfect. We were perfect. What happened to us? Why are we broken now?

All kids, at this stage in their lives, need someone to talk to. Typically parents are not involved. Kids tend to choose other people to help sort out complex issues, usually friends who are as clueless as they are. If kids aren't lucky enough to have someone to talk to and help them sort out their problems, then the real problems begin, as their sense of judgment as to what is important and what isn't, and what is right or wrong will be made with no adult input or perspective. This is a frightening situation, which is prevalent on a worldwide basis. Sometimes it's hard to solve a problem with the same mind that created it, noted Albert Einstein.

This is the most important and troubling stage in kids' lives. Not all teenagers are searching for answers about the bigger issues in life, but for those who are, this is a really desperate time. Many of those kids feel a total lack of hope, as they can see themselves as worthless because they don't know who they are and how they can achieve happiness, when so little of it is surrounding them. Some teenagers are keen enough to spot fake happiness, and fake happiness doesn't count.

Without someone to help us sort out important issues in our life, we are really in a difficult position. We need to have things bounced off people who can help us with their perspective. Of course we need to seek out people whom we trust and who have lived their life successfully, (according to what we think a successful life is). Kids are shy and won't let go of their inner feelings easily, and oftentimes we only hear about our own children or their friends from other people, typically after situations have reached a critical level. I guess it has always been this way. I am hopeful that things can change for the better in the future.

The counseling was useful for Evan and seemed to help him figure out what was going on in his life, although the pain persisted. Just before his 13th birthday, I *had* to give him his present early, because we were so worried about his mental state. Evan finally got the Gibson Les Paul guitar that he had been wanting for so long. It seemed to make him only slightly happier.

> *"I never realized how much alike Evan and I actually were. We were both going through periods of self-exploration, confusion and even self hate. We both had a love for sports and music. He expressed himself through pen and paper, as I do."*

Evan once said to me "What's the point of living if you don't feel alive"? I stood in silence, not knowing an answer, not one that was right at least. That's because there is no point to living if you don't feel alive. I cry myself to sleep because I can't stand the way anything is going. Evan would listen to me, if only here were here."
— a friend

Evan was undergoing a tough, critical analysis of who he was, who his real friends were, how he fit in, and in which group he fit into. So much pain, startling in its intensity. Those of us who were close to him wanted it to stop. It was as if he was in the throes of wrestling demons inside him. What was the hurry? Why was it so important to cram so much passion into the process of delving into such matters that most kids deal with later on in life, typically with less intensity? Evan had such a voracious appetite for learning and exploring; it was impossible for him to just dismiss a thought, belief, or a concept without really thinking about it, including subjects such as evil, Marilyn Manson, good, God, and just about everything else.

He was really into Marilyn Manson, and we thought it was for the wrong reasons, like being attracted to evil. We found out, talking to Evan's psychologist, that Evan thought Marilyn Manson was only doing what he was doing as an act—that he didn't really care for him at all, at the end of his period of "observation." We were relived, to say the least, but it showed us that Evan's thought process was to reject nothing initially without being open minded about it. I think now, that this is actually healthy, and consistent with the way we brought him up: "*find your own way and don't believe everything people tell you,*" which obviously he didn't.

During Evan's period of fascination with Marilyn Manson, I took him to a Manson concert. We both had a great time; the stage was awesome. Manson rose about 30 feet in the air at one point, on an elevator like contraption, which added to the overall effect he tried so hard to perfect. The music was really loud and much appreciated by the fans, and the fans themselves were certainly part of the show, with so many of them dressed in their best black outfits, or in other outrageous styles. I'm really glad I took him.

November 19

Evan painted his room black. We were at first surprised, but since it was his room, we let him. It actually looked rather elegant after he took down his band posters and assorted junk that was hung on his walls prior to the black treatment. He "borrowed" a great looking gothic mirror that Nancy had bought for the downstairs bathroom, painted it gold and hung it in his room. Evan was so proud of his black room and delighted that we would let him paint it in his favorite color. His friends were suitably impressed, and many of the parents who came to our house couldn't fathom how we could let Evan paint his room black. They just didn't "get it" and might not ever get it, although I hope that one day they will let go of their concepts of how things "should be," and let their kids live a little.

One of Evan's friends wanted to paint his room black, both in memory and honor of Evan, but his mom convinced him that dark blue would look better and that was as far as she could go. I think Evan would have refused and said "*black or nothing*." You just can't compromise your life away and expect to be happy, although certainly comprise is appropriate in many situations that face us. Sometimes, it isn't right to compromise, and I think we intuitively know when those times are. The trick is being to be bold enough not to comprise when we know we shouldn't.

The school issues wouldn't go away. We tried to coax Evan into getting better grades: no TV during the week, maybe a few bribes, but eventually though we realized the only true way to get to him to study was to tell him that it was *his* education and it was up to him to prepare for the future. If he wanted to get good grades so that he could go to a good college, he needed to start getting good grades now, because bad habits are hard to break. He really wanted us to bug him about getting good grades, but we didn't want to. He was actually mad at us for not being "normal" and yelling at him if he didn't do well in school, like all his friends' parents did. Not doing well for Evan was mostly all B's and a few C's. It was up to him. He had to make the internal commitment to buckle down and do what he had to do.

Evan's girlfriend Elizabethe, who was a straight A student, inspired him to really try hard and make the Honor Roll the last grading period of seventh grade. He hadn't made the Honor Roll all year and he wanted to test the theory that he was capable of making the Honor Roll if he put forth the effort. He wanted to understand *"Can I do this or not?"* He wouldn't really know unless he tried, and he hadn't really tried. It was easy for him to say he was smart but he wanted to know what would happen if he put in the effort into his schoolwork. *"I could have made it if I really tried,"* people say. Evan decided to see if that was true after all.

Evan raised himself to the Honor Roll for the first time that year. Of course, he was really proud of himself, and I began to get the feeling from him that he now knew he could achieve whatever he wanted to. It made him feel really powerful. I was watching and witnessing a change in Evan that I had never seen before. Such power being awakened. It excited and delighted Evan. Seventh grade was starting to become a pivotal year for him. Nancy explained to him at the end of the school year that we really weren't concerned about his grades because he was learning so much about himself, and learning about yourself is educational. However, there were changes going on that affected Evan and the world around him.

Evan finally won the battle that was raging inside of him. The dark cold winter was behind him, and a new life was beginning, opening up at the same time the earth was opening up her flowers. Evan basically figured out his role and who he was. He was Evan, simply put, and Evan could be anything he wanted to be. He could dress any way he wanted to and still be friends with anyone and any group and any person he wanted to. That is "real freedom." I saw the process happen to Evan, and it was as if a revelation came to him and said "just be yourself." You don't have to try so hard to be someone or something other than who you are. Appreciate yourself and celebrate being you. It's what you are, not what you aren't. Just being yourself is fine. However, just being yourself sometimes isn't enough to get you where you want to be.

This process of understanding came to Evan after a lengthy, intense search, which is typically how we find things. I would imagine if Evan hadn't been searching so hard, he wouldn't have found what he was looking for, although at the beginning of his search he (or we) cannot know how the search will turn out. Nevertheless the search is crucial. What would have happened if Evan had never searched at all? I think we all know that answer.

IM Conversations

This is an Instant Messenger conversation between Evan and one of his friends that took place during 7th grade toward the end of the school year, showing his own realization and ability to change.

Tom: whats up
Evan: nothing much
Evan: im a sellout?
Tom: yes
Evan: since when
Tom: since middle of last year
Evan: explain
Tom: beginning of last year, you were the ANTI-preppy
Evan: dude, the preppies are nice
Tom: you hated ever single preppy in our school
Evan: ur friends with them too
Tom: no kidding
Evan soo
Tom: again no kidding
Evan: doesn't that make u a "non-anti-preppy"?
Tom: you hated them
Evan: yeah
Evan: for no reason
Tom: I never was an anti preppy
Evan: yeah?
Tom: ive always been friends with them you werent
Evan: so what, are you a sellout?
Tom: you hated them
Evan: so what?
Tom: that was why you were really cool
Evan: I didn't have a reason
Evan: im sorry u don't think im cool anymore just because I don't hate people for no reason anymore
Tom: that was why you were so cool
Evan: it doesn't change me
Tom: yeah yeah yeah

Evan: im still the same
Evan: just look different
Tom: that exactly it, your not the same at all
Evan: im different, people change

It takes effort to achieve your dreams, and there are no shortcuts. Evan remarked to his friends in his many Instant Messenger conversations that it was important to try and be nice to people, and that's the way to make friends and have people like you. It required some work, which he was prepared to do. That was Evan's way, do what you needed to do. He wanted and needed people to like him, and he figured out how, just like his mom. He realized that it was his responsibility to act first and be nice first—and not wait for others to be nice to him, as some of his friends thought. Of course those friends of Evan's who were waiting for everyone to be nice to them first had very few friends. I don't think it was a coincidence.

Evan also saved this Instant Messenger conversation. It was a conversation with one of his friends about some problems the friend was having. The name of his friend has been changed.

11.01

The entire IM session was quite lengthy, about 7 written pages in all. I am just including excerpts so that you get the essence of the communication.

Evan: ur in pain?
Bob: I'm always in pain
Evan: from what?
Bob: physically, mentally, I'm always hurt
Evan: from what
Bob: people don't like me
Evan: be nicer
Bob: I hate every soul that has put me down.
Evan: dude, I have been put down by everyone, even my friends
Evan: just who do u want 2 like you?
Bob: what does it matter, People look at me and run in fear

Evan: but they don't have to. just make more of an effort to be nice

Bob: I don't

Evan: they just think you are mean and shit. Be nice to them. When u see them just be like hey or something

Evan: its not much but its enough to make them nicer to you

Bob: I've tried! They just look at me like im an asswhole

Evan: do it again

Evan : don't give up yet

Bob: look at the preppy kids, they all hate me

Evan: yea. They used to all hate me

Evan: be nicer to them

Evan: like really nice

Bob: since the first grade all people have done is judge me, hate me, and treat me like shit

Bob: I'm big so they called me fat

Bob: whats wrong with being big?

Evan: girls don't like it I guess

Bob: Its not that its cuz I look mean

Evan: u have 2 make up in your personality what ur missing in your looks I guess…

Bob: I like my look, I can be nice! I can be really nice…. if people are nice to me

Evan: they wont be. U have 2 make the effort

Evan: just be nicer to them

Bob: a lot of people really hate me don't they?

Evan: they just hate what they don't understand

Evan: they just don't know u so they stereotype you

Bob: they only hate the bad in me

Evan then brings on a bunch of other people on IM and asks them what they think about Bob. It was like a large conference call/therapy session. Most reply Bob is sort of nice but can also be mean— but also funny and nice. Bob is really surprised to see that some people like him.

The conversation continues:

Evan: it didn't matter what I looked like cuz im ugly and they were nice 2 me

Evan: I was just nice 2 them

Bob: but then I was nice and they were nice 2 me

Bob: im too intimidating, im different from everyone else

Evan: I was but then I was nice and they were nice 2 me

Bob: I don't know how to be nice

Evan: try

Evan: just be like hi whats up, how are u, what are u doin this weekend, what did u get on ur report card, shit like that

Bob: no one has ever been nice to me

Evan: yea, be nice 2 them

Evan: try it!

Bob: I don't think I have one friend

Evan: ull never know until u try

Evan: Im ur friend

Evan: theres one

Evan: ur my friend

Bob: oh

Bob: a friend is someone who cares about you

Bob: I don't have any

Evan: don't kill ur self

Bob: what is my reason to live

Evan: u don't know what your future holds for you

Evan: live to find out

Evan: u could be really smart if u tried

Bob: Im holding a cross in my hand now

Evan: why?

Bob: every night I hold it and pray that tomorrow will be better, that people will understand me, that people will care about me! But it never comes

Evan: care about them

Evan: u have 2 make the effort

Evan: now

Evan: they care about u but u just didn't know it

Evan: everyone thinks u can be nice

Evan: be nice
Bob: yeah they would care if I died only because I died. If they care then y do they act like they don't
Evan: they will like u
Evan: how do they act like that, they don't?
Bob: they make fun of me, treat me like im dirt, like im not human
Evan: give them a chance
Bob: I have my whole life and I just get kicked around
Evan: u have your whole life in front of u
Evan: ur only 13 and u have no idea what will happen
Bob: yeah and look where I am heading
Evan: I was heading there 2
Evan: I changed tho. I figured if I was nice 2 them they'll be nice 2 me
Bob: yeah but you have a girlfriend, someone who cares, I don't
Evan: im your friend, I care if you die, so there
Bob: yeah, if I die! Not if im alive
Evan: I care that ur alive 2
Bob: no girls or boys care about me
Evan: I do
Bob: no teachers do
Evan: cuz u don't try
Evan: u could be smart but u don't try
Evan: just try, set goals and shit, try and live up 2 them
Evan: get help
Evan: tell your mom ur not happy and she will get someone, that's what I did
Evan: im better now
Evan: I'll call her and tell her u need help
Bob: but im not happy, im never happy, I don't know how to be happy
Evan: then learn
Evan: find someone u can talk2
Bob: no one wants to talk to me
Bob: you have to tell some people for me
Evan: I'll email my buddy list and u can IM them and shit

Bob: I cry myself to sleep every night man!!!
Evan: that's wicked sad
Bob: you hafta tell people
Evan: I will
Evan then emails this conversation to all the people on his buddy list (150+). It's a cry of help from Bob.
Final words: Bob: I can't even ask a girl out, im afraid
Evan: be nice 2 her

I had heard about this conversation from Evan, but I didn't realize that he had saved it on his computer. We found it when we were going through his files after his death. It must have meant something to Evan to save it. I have been talking to Bob and Bob comes over sometimes and continues to talk about life and his struggle to find some answers to his questions. Nancy and I really like Bob, and are committed to staying in touch and helping him as much as possible. It would make Evan very happy.

Here is another perspective;

> *"When I first met Evan, I noticed that he was really nice. He didn't judge people before he got to know them. Everyone in the group liked him and he really communicated well. He always helped people out who were having problems at home and with school.*
>
> *Once he helped me with a problem that I was having with my grandparents. Evan told me that I had to look at all of the positive things that were coming out of the situation. Ever since then, I have learned to focus on the good parts of my situation and set aside the bad.*
>
> *I never really thanked him for the problem afterwards, but if I had, I would have thanked him for helping me out. I wish I could have thanked him or returned the favor somehow, but now that I don't have the chance to do that, I want to somehow commemorate his life.*

The way I am going to remember Evan is by what he said to me. He helped me look at situations differently and now problems are easier to solve. I will always be grateful for Evan's help."
— Friend's Life Is Remembered": Article written for the Groton High School paper.

December 2

Evan was also trying to perfect his look and one thing that really bothered him was teenage acne. He wanted to find the cure for it, at least for himself.

During this period, Evan's skin was breaking out and it caused him much embarrassment. He was really into finding a way to end teenage acne, at least Evan's teenage acne. We began the usual visits to the dermatologist, had the usual things prescribed; the acne washes, the Triaz, the RetinA, the oral antibiotics. Nothing much was working. But once summer came, he decided to go off the antibiotics and try it 'natural.' He had asked for books from the library on nutrition because he wanted to see what was the best food to eat for getting in shape and having good skin.

After much reading he decided to stay away from sugar and fatty foods, drink lots of water, eat lots of fruit and vegetables, and just about lived on protein shakes. The blender was always whirring. He made sure he kept his face scrupulously clean, especially after exercising (this could mean 3 showers a day) got daily sun and followed a skin regimen only a chemist could have designed. Needless to say, his skin looked great due to his unbelievable will power. I'm not sure I have ever been as dedicated to anything in my life as Evan was to clearing up his skin.
— Mom

As Evan began to understand who he was, he began to become more and more involved reaching out to his friends who were suffering from life questions and just plain old teenage problems. Evan was trying to alleviate their pain by listening to them and giving advice. His friends, who had great respect for Evan, did listen to his words. I have many letters that testify to Evan's help in numerous situations, although most of those that he had helped remarked that Evan probably didn't understand how much he helped, because they never told him.

One of Evan's friends told me that he felt that Evan was the most respected kid in middle school simply for who and what he was. Only after Evan died did his friends come forth and start to share their thoughts about him. It's a shame Evan didn't know how they felt sooner, but it's okay. I think he would have been very proud of himself and happy that he could be of assistance to his friends, whom he cared about so deeply. Also, since Evan knew that he had the ability to help; it was sort of an obligation that he knew he had to fulfill.

> *"My parents knew I was unhappy, but I never wanted their help. One night I was planning on making all my pain go away. For some reason I went online and Evan was on. I don't really know why I decided to tell him this, but I think it was because I knew he would understand. He reminded me of my friends, family, and everyone else that cared for me. There was one thing that really hit home for me, he said that he would be incredibly upset if I left this world that way, he said he loved me. My parents always say that, but coming from a boy (especially Evan) I felt like it was true. At that moment, I decided life is too precious to take away on my own.*
>
> *Evan was one of my best friends I ever had, although I don't think he ever knew that. I hope he knew he saved my life."*
> *— a friend*

Another in a series of letters we received:

> *"The first time I went over to your house in Washington, D.C. Nancy took Evan and I grocery shopping with her. She bought us Doritos, and the entire time Evan and I were in the car we had contests on who could keep their breath hot the longest by scarfing down Doritos at top speed. That was the very first impression of my great friend Evan.*
>
> *I remember Evan's great advice two years ago (2000), it was not to worry about the clothes you wear, it doesn't matter what others think, the trick is finding your own happiness, and being comfortable with yourself.*
>
> *Last year it was don't wus out in life. If u are gonna live, u might as well do it balls out or else there is no point. Live life to the fullest, live the way Evan did.*
>
> *I remember Evan teaching me how to blow a snot rocket. At the time, Evan's huge snot rocket blowing skills were most amazing thing I have ever witnessed, and I was completely blown away. He went over the correct form with me, and then the correct snorting techniques to maximize air time.*
>
> *Evan was an amazing friend and person. He had a huge impact on my life, and I will always love him. I am relieved to say I told him how much I appreciated his advice, what a great friend he was, and how much I loved him before it was too late.*
>
> *I will never forget Evan, ever. I cannot believe such a horrible thing happened to him of all people. I mean Evan Holofcener, he was the one person I viewed to be invincible, he was always huge, strong and tough, and the greatest friend ever. Evan, I love you, you are the greatest friend ever."*
> *— old friend from D.C.*

This letter was sent to Evan from a casual 7th grade acquaintance:

> *"You are the coolest guy I have ever met. I have never really felt like a somebody. I don't have many friends, and I have definitively never been considered a cool person. Last year in geography class you made me feel so cool. You treated and talked to me like I was just a plain cool kid. Thanx for treating me nice, although I am an ugly, social outcast. I'm so sorry that you're gone. It wasn't your time. I wish I had gotten to know you better. I'd always wanted to know you better. I guess life was kind of hard for you. The poem you wrote about wearing a mask, that's how I feel. I am not a happy kid, but I have to get up in the place and put on a mask that makes me look like I'm happy. I'm so sorry. I love you so much Evan. I will never forget you. Although we were not close friends, I wish I had been. You were so cool. I miss you so much. Your family has such a great guy to be proud of. I'm gonna miss you so much. My family doesn't understand me much, but I know you would understand. I love and miss you. Hope you are happy where ever you are."*

The following letter was sent to us by one of Evan's closest friends:

> *"I am really bad! I miss you so much! I am crying now that how sad I am. I am miserable! I still can't believe it had to be you! I hope you can hear me wherever you are. You were one of my best friends who I will never forget. If there was one person in the world who I want to talk to it is you. I really wanted to dance with you at the dances this year. You were the first person I danced with! I wanted you to be my first everything. I miss you so much. You have helped me realize so much that I would have never realized without you. You were the most perfect person I knew. I could trust you with any secret of mine! You were so sweet. Whenever I needed an honest answer, I could ask you. You were even nice to my brothers when I told you not to be. It is sometimes the littlest things in life that matter a lot.*
>
> *No one knows how sad I am. The only thing that will make me feel better is you coming back. I know that will never happen but I*

> *wish there was something to change this or a time machine and not let you go on that bike trip. I have so many questions that don't have any answers. I wish you were here to help me. Is it really worth living, I know the answer is YES, but there is so much pain. You were a hero for everyone that knew you and for everyone who didn't want to know you. Every one looked up to you. Will I ever see you again? One of the biggest questions I have is, are you watching us, are you still here? I have been wondering that. I don't believe in stuff like having haloes but it feels like you're here."*

Although Evan found the light at the end of the tunnel it didn't mean that he was in perfect peace at all times. This is a really important point for me to relate. Evan didn't find perfect happiness, which would have lasted the rest of his life He would have always had to try his absolute best in everything he was doing in order to get the most out of it. This wasn't a Disney ending where everybody lives happily ever after. This was real life, and real death. Children as well as adults still struggle with identity issues, life issues, and girl and boy issues, which will continue to cause us pain as we live our lives. It's how we try our best with the cards we are dealt that makes the difference in our lives, and the lives of others.

> *"Ever since Evan's death I have realized a few things about life that I never really saw b4. For example, Evan did in 13 years what most people do in 40 or more. His life was packed with emotion, athletics, travel, friends, family, and other things that people rarely get to experience on that level. In doing so, I think he almost "overachieved" if you will."*
> *— a friend*

Evan was also withdrawing from his family during much of seventh grade. He didn't share his thoughts with us, which he had readily done his whole life. No, this new world was strictly his. He wasn't talking to Nancy or me about things that were going on in his life. He did talk a bit, but not about issues concerning him personally. That sharing, about his ideas and thoughts, were confined primarily to his friends. Evan's girlfriend, Elizabethe, was the object of his affection for six months, unusual in its duration and intensity for middle school. He and Elizabethe would talk on the phone for hours. Once, they had a nine-hour phone conversation. When I asked what they talked about after the conversation ended, Evan said *"nothing much"* with a big smile on his face. We were glad he found such happiness in his new life as an independent being. He made all his own meals, did his own laundry, could fix anything that needed fixing, and didn't need help with his homework.

Evan really wanted us to build an apartment in our backyard so that he could live in it by himself. He wanted his own life, an independent life. His dream was to go to Lawrence Academy, (a local private high school) on a hockey scholarship and live in the dorms—though we lived less than two miles away. I knew he would have gotten the scholarship, and we would have let him dorm there.

Evan continued to write poetry and continued with his drawings. Both were quite good, particularly his poetry for someone so young. His lyrics were incredibly sensitive for someone who was seemingly so tough on the exterior, which is the image he projected to some of his friends. There were many things we were to find out that we didn't know about Evan. His friends and teachers saw a different side of Evan, particularly his girl friends, who saw the more poetic, sensitive side of him. They were kind enough to write notes to us after Evan's death, sharing private moments and incidents that continue to delight his mom and me.

Evan's 7th Grade English teacher wrote this letter to the editor to the *Groton Herald.*

> *In Memory of Evan Holofcener*
>
> *Labor Day weekend of 2001 was the most disturbing, tragic, tear-soaked weekend of my life. Waking up Sunday morning September 2nd to news on the radio that 13 year old, Evan Holofcener, a Groton eight grader, had died in a bicycle accident was too surreal. The news pierced my heart with such pain and sickness that my emotions altered any holiday plans I*

had scheduled.

Evan was a student in my seventh grade English class during the 2001-2002 school year, and he was a vital member of my homeroom. Throughout the year, Evan and I talked a lot about the future and success; he became an inspiration to me. Evan also became a vibrant part of my student family, an academic bloomer, and a brother in youthful friendship.

Evan's writing was inspired, creative, and thoughtful; his poetry was alive with symbolic energy. I particularly remember his artistic talent in the various projects he created for presentation to the class. Evan shared his music with me, and he repeatedly shared his thoughts on literature with the class during class discussion times. Evan and I had developed over the 183 days of the school year his plan for life improvement, and his incredible desire to be on guard to choose the right path throughout his life. I will keep close to my heart his thoughts that flowed from his year-end portfolio project; a project he introduced with pictures of he and his guitar.

The incredibly unfair, untimely, and incomprehensible death of Evan Holofcener is a loss to our world, a loss to the future of the needy society in which we live, and specifically a loss to the students and adults of the town of Groton. As I begin a new teaching position teaching high school in another community, I symbolically dedicate my year to Evan. In all that I teach and in all that I share individually with students, I will do so in the spirit that Evan Holofcener so powerfully showed me.

My heart is very, very sick. My faith allows me to move on by giving me the understanding that I will see Evan someday so that we can share poetry, music and spirited conversation.

You changed my life as a teacher and as a man, Evan.

Sincerely
Phillip LeFevre

Evan wrote this poem to Elizabethe. It turned out to be a misunderstanding.

Love lost-
I remember being in your arms
Looking in your eyes
Never once wanting to look away
Under the stars we laid
Dreaming sweet dreams
Of me and you
Together forever
Some dreams come true
And others I guess…
Are meant to stay dreams
Love
I try
Not to think of how you made me feel
I don't want to remember that
I still love you
I don't want to see that I care
I don't want to look at the blue roses
You never forgot
They were my favorite
Wilting in my room
From you
A small card saying "I love you"
Hate
I want to hate you
For leaving me
Leaving me here all alone
Hate you for loving him
For not loving me
Resent
I resent each time you hold him
Hold him like you held me
Resent each kiss you place on his lips
Kiss him like you kissed me
Jealousy

Jealous of him
Of each "I love you"
You whisper sweetly in his ear
The red roses
You lay in his hands
And not mine
Missing
I miss you
Miss the smile you kept on my face
Miss the way you kissed me
Miss your soft colored eyes

December 5

During seventh grade, Evan was growing very strong and tall and delighted in his muscular form, and his size 12 shoes. He grew to 5'10."This past summer while in serious training for hockey he ended up losing 16 pounds and gaining significant muscle mass, which gave him a really muscled, sculpted body. While he talked on the phone, typically in the basement, he would be using our weight station, doing crunches and lifting weights. He would do this for hours at a time. We were watching him in amazement, saying things like, *"Eat more food. Take it easy— what's your hurry? Don't push yourself so hard."*

He would just smile and ask us to punch him in the stomach because he finally had a "six pack" and, his stomach was as hard as a rock. He would measure his biceps and yell out "13 ½."I didn't know if that was good, but when he flexed his biceps they looked and felt like solid rocks. It was last summer that Evan could finally beat me in arm wrestling, something he had been trying to do for years. I was delighted he finally beat me. It was really important to him, and I am glad he got that satisfaction before it was too late.

Evan enjoyed the fact that he was going to be a tall, good looking, blond, green- eyed, athletic, and artistic person. Somehow, from a convoluted idea of his Mom's heritage, he believed he was descended from Lithuania, and thought himself to be the classic image of a

German youth. We couldn't understand his feelings and to this day still don't. That was part of Evan's mystique.

Sports

December 6

Evan started playing ice hockey in the winter of fourth grade. Initially, he had to enroll in the learn to skate program, which put this big nine-year-old in the same classes as the 3-5 year olds, since in New England, hockey programs start early in life. One dad remarked that it took a lot of courage for this big fourth grader to get on the ice with such small kids, and said that his own kids would never have had the courage to do that. That was Evan's way. Do what you have to do.

> *"On a personal level, I also have fond memories of Evan. Soon after the Holofceners moved to Groton, Evan was enrolled in the GJHA (Groton Junior Hockey Association) and, since he had no prior ice skating experience, he was assigned to the Mosquito program. I happened to be the Mosquito Coordinator during his first season, and much to my surprise, Evan could skate the moment he hit the ice. Since Evan was an athletic kid and had a lot of inline skating experience at his prior home, Washington, D.C. the "push and glide" motion seemed to come naturally. I should mention that Evan was 9 years old at that time in a program of mostly 5 and 6 year-olds so the social climate was less than ideal.*
>
> *However Evan* ***really*** *wanted to play hockey and made astonishing progress. By January we were able to place him on a travel team with players in his own age group and he was able to play competitively. I know that Evan loved hockey and kept working hard to be the best player that he could be. When I think back on my association with GJHA in various roles, I cannot think of anything that gives me greater pleasure than Evan's dedication and skills development that first season."*
>
> *— hockey dad*

His first and second years of playing hockey were erratic in terms of his game performances. I was never sure which Evan would show up for the game: the passionate, play hard every second Evan, or the Evan who barely tried. Of course, as a parent, I used to ask him after every game how he thought he did, which I thought was a much better way of talking about the game, rather than me telling him how I thought he did. He usually said he sucked, even when I thought he played well. We had the usual talks about trying your hardest, but nothing seemed to penetrate.

Once, I took my video camera to a game and captured Evan's every move. When I showed him the film, he was shocked. He noticed that he wasn't really playing hard— and that he really thought he could have done better. This was not my purpose in taping the game. I simply thought he would simply enjoy seeing himself on film. After that, things changed. I never had to say another word, because he starting trying harder and harder to play his best. And he kept getting better and better: his slap shot, which was developed naturally, just happened. It became the talk of the league and his teammates, and even opposing teams would compliment Evan on his "wicked slap shot."

> *"One instance that stands out in my mind is the time our team was playing a game, and I was standing beside the father of an opposing player. When Evan wound up to take one of his famous slap shots, this father was awestruck. I remember that he saw Evan's name on the back of his jersey and he remarked "His name should not be Holofcener, it should be Howitzer."*
> *— hockey teammate*

> *"My most memorable time with Evan was in a hockey game when we played together on PeeWee 2 last year. Evan fired a slap shot from the point, it hit the goalie's helmet and I got it and scored the game-winning goal on the deflection. Evan skated towards me and picked me up as high in the air as he could and said "You did it Steve."We were both so excited. I will never forget that game. I will never forget Evan's wicked slap shot. I will never forget Evan."*
> *— hockey teammate*

His hockey coach, Chuck White was very inspirational and he helped Evan so much by providing him the freedom that he needed at that time. He would encourage Evan to shoot the puck any time he wanted to. This was partly because Evan had developed a very good slap shot that that scored goals, while playing defense. But there was more to it than that however, it wasn't simply that Coach White wanted to win every game; he wanted to get the best out of each player. *"Let go*" his coach would say, something I have been saying to Evan all of his life. *"Don't be afraid to shoot*" he was told. *"Don't be afraid to make a mistake*."

It took Evan some time to understand what Coach White was saying. Then he started applying his understanding, and things began to change. The passion that had been dormant for so long emerged along with the freedom that inherently resides in each one of us. When passion enters your life, your life will change. I will never forget the lessons Coach White taught Evan. They were life lessons that went well beyond hockey. Evan loved his coach, and I know the feeling was mutual.

Last summer, Evan learned that he was placed on the Bantam 2 hockey team, a really good team. His coach, for the second year in a row, was going to be Chuck White. Evan was ecstatic about playing for Coach White again. Eighth grade was going to be fantastic!

There were two practices before eighth grade started in late August. At one of the practices I was watching Evan shooting slap shots. Last year his slap shot was very powerful but the accuracy wasn't so great. I watched him hit eight out of ten shots at one of the practice sessions. I told him that I thought his shooting had really improved. He said that his shot was off. At first I thought he was kidding, but I then realized that his new experience of life was providing him with such power and focus that he thought he could do things almost perfectly. The experience he was having seemed to provide him with almost unlimited capability. I could only wonder what he was feeling and experiencing.

In November of 2001, the Massachusetts Hockey Bantam A State finals was played at the Groton School. The best Bantam A teams in the State competed, with the winner going to the Nationals in Florida. The tournament was dedicated to Evan by Mark Frederickson, his first hockey coach, who was Co-Chairman of the event.

DEDICATION

Evan Holofcener

This tournament is dedicated to the memory of Evan Holofcener, an extraordinary member of the Groton Junior Hockey family who will never be forgotten. Earlier this fall, Evan was the victim of a tragic accident, struck by a motor vehicle while he was riding his bicycle on Farmer's Row. Evan, 14, was a talented member of the Groton Bantam 2 hockey team, known for his passion for hockey and his blistering slapshot. An accomplished guitar player, he loved music with the same passion. He was raised in a close, loving family who taught him well and marveled at his talents, perseverance and charisma. We are honored to dedicate this tournament to Evan Holofcener, a wonderful friend, teammate, son and brother. Evan, you will always be in our hearts.

"Mark, Nancy and Ryan,
Thank you for agreeing to let us honor Evan in our small way this weekend. My team is wearing EH22 (Evan's hockey number)-and they have never played better in their lives. He is our inspiration."
— Mark Frederickson

MASSACHUSETTS HOCKEY
STATE FINALS
Bantam A National Bound

Evan Holofcener
1987-2001

November 9, 10 and 11, 2001

Hosted By
Groton Junior Hockey Association

The photo of the hockey player on the cover of the program is Evan winding up to take one of his famous slap shots

(Evan was 13, not 14)

Coach White has spearheaded a Memorial Fund for Evan, to sponsor kids who want to play hockey. So far, thousands of dollars have been raised. The money will either be used to fund a college scholarship for a Groton Hockey player, or it will go to sponsor local kids who want to play hockey but cannot afford the $1000 annual cost. I think it would make Evan the happiest to make it possible for many kids learn to play hockey, because it brought so much joy to him.

This season, 2001/2002, the entire Bantam 2 season has been dedicated to Evan. All the members of team including the coaches wear an EH patch on their game jerseys, placed directly over their hearts. At the beginning of every game the coaches talk to the players about Evan and how much he meant to them and tell the players to try hard and win for Evan, and of course for themselves. When the team comes out of huddles, instead of yelling *"Go Groton Go,"* which has been the traditional cheer, they now come out of the huddle and yell *"Evan."* The team plays each and every game for Evan. Members of the Bantam 3 team, which includes some kids who played with Evan last year, also have the EH patches. Recently, a dad from the Bantam 3 team shared with me that his son told him how proud he was to wear the EH patch on his game jersey. As you can imagine, I was deeply touched.

An "EH" sticker has now been placed on Ryan's Squirt 2 hockey team's helmets. Of course Ryan proudly wears the EH patch. The EH patch is being worn by Evan's lacrosse team, a sport Evan was just learning to play. The local area football team had dedicated their season to Evan. They too are wearing EH stickers on their helmets and painted EH on their faces at each game, in greasepaint. The football team won the 2001 State Championship, and the game ball was given to Ryan affixed with the EH sticker worn by the players.

December 8

I attended my first Bantam 2 game to watch Evan's team playing. For some reason, I needed to go, primarily to show my support for the team that was dedicating their season to Evan. It was both easier and harder than I had anticipated. Once Evan's team scored their first goal, every player, including those on the bench, skated over to where Ryan and I were sitting in the stands. One of the players threw me the hockey puck. I immediately gave it to Ryan. The entire skating rink erupted in applause. They were really cheering for Evan. It was quite an emotional evening, although, sadly, I was getting more used to evenings like this.

I was really glad Ryan was there to see how much people cared for his brother. After Evan's team won 5-0, I went into the locker room, and thanked all the players for remembering Evan this season. I wanted them to know how deeply touched our family was and is for their remembrance of, and their dedication to Evan.

The girl's eighth grade basketball team have EH written on their shoes and they too are playing the season for Evan. It is all so overwhelming, and we are so proud and touched by the outpouring of affection and love for Evan by so many of his peers. Evan would be embarrassed, happy, and surprised at all the attention he is getting, but I think he mostly would be surprised.

In December of each year for the past 24 years, there is a large Christmas Hockey Tournament held in Groton, where the best teams in the Northeast play for the championship. Last year, Evan's old PeeWee team, under Coach White, won their division's championship. In 2001 the tournament was dedicated to Evan and there was a beautiful ceremony to retire his game jersey. The jersey was encased in glass and was hung in the Groton School's new hockey rink.The plaque accompanying his game jersey says:

Evan Maxwell Holofcener 1988-2001
In loving memory of our friend and teammate
who lived every moment, played every shift with passion.
Your inspiration will never be forgotten.

Hundreds of Evan's friends and fellow hockey players filled the Groton School hockey rink to honor him and to pay their respects to a kid who deserved respect. Both for who he was and what he accomplished. The entire high school hockey team, along with Evan's old hockey teams were on the ice in uniform. One by one, Evan's old team mates silently skated up to the dedication area where Nancy,

Ryan, and I were seated on the ice next to the as yet unveiled jersey and gave Nancy an individual rose. Her arms were filled with roses by the end of the night. More crying. How many tears are in this body anyway?

Chuck White was the emcee and couldn't have done a better job letting people know how special Evan was, thus the reason for retiring his jersey, although virtually everyone in the rink knew how special Evan was anyway. Nancy gave one of the roses to Ryan and asked him to give it to Evan's girlfriend Elizabethe, who was in the stands. That would have made Evan really happy.

Music:

Evan *loved* music. It was part of him and he was part of it. When he was 10 he took his first guitar lessons at Daddy's Junky Music in Nashua, New Hampshire. The music lessons were hard, but he was willing to put in the effort to learn the songs and the chord structures and began to learn how to read music. At first, things moved slowly. Then, Evan started to learn the lessons for the week in a very short period of time. Something was happening. He progressed very rapidly, learning song after song. His love of metal music began to grow by leaps and bounds. Metallica was one of his earliest favorites, along with Korn and Limp Bizkit, moving on to Slipknot, StaticX, Pantera and MudVayne. I hated the lyrics of many of the bands, and had a very difficult time allowing him to buy CDs with such dire messages.

At some point, you have to let go and hope the parenting you have provided will give your child the lessons needed to let them enjoy the pounding music, take the lyrics for what they were, and understand that the words are sometimes only meant to shock and provoke. I still didn't like him listening to those lyrics, but he was given the opportunity to both accept as well as reject thoughts and ideas. That was his right and privilege. We didn't however let Evan buy his first Parental Advisory CD until he was twelve. That's the way we raised him, and I don't have any regrets, at least about this subject.

By the end of the second year of guitar lessons, Evan outgrew the teaching structure and began to improvise and learn independently. He spent countless hours downloading TAB, and songs from Napster and later from Morpheus. His appetite was voracious for learning new material. Evan said that it only took him one or two times to pick up almost any song last summer, (which I witnessed). His passion for music began to play a bigger role in his life. He was always experimenting with various chord structures and had his second guitar; a Peavy Predator Plus, tuned to some new string arrangement it seemed like every week. He was working on getting a seven-string guitar sound on his six-string guitar. He was also spending more and more time with his acoustic guitar, and was working on playing softer songs, which he said the girls liked.

"I always enjoyed his lessons, not just because he was a good player, but because of his positive attitude, intelligence, and openness. He seemed very well adjusted and articulate to the point that I would often forget that I was talking to a 12 or 13 year old.

One thing that impressed me about Evan was his interest and inquisitiveness about the guitar and music, which for some strange reason is rare with most students. Evan would oftentimes bring up questions about guitars, equipment, Metallica, Hendrix, etc., which I enjoyed talking about and is sometimes as important to know as notes and chords.

Musically, I enjoyed the lessons because of Evan's open minded attitude as well as his talent. I always felt that I could show him a song or different style of music and he would give it 100% even if he wasn't 100% into it.

The clearest memory I have of Evan is from his first recital in which he played Aura Lee. By the way I get nervous for the students because you never know what is going to happen in front of an audience, regardless of how well one knows the music. Anyway, we started playing and Evan sounded good and solid, not nervous as I knew he was. He played the whole song perfectly and just after finishing turned around and looked at me with a huge, triumphant smile which completely expressed his happiness and pride and I think surprise with his performance. I can still see that smile, it's etched in my memory, I think it will always be."
— Don, Evan's guitar teacher

One really fond memory I have is taking Evan to rock concerts. His taste in music basically ran from metal to heavy metal. He really wanted to go to the concerts where his favorite bands were playing, to see the bands in person and perhaps learn some new guitar techniques. The importance of him going to concerts was not overlooked. The concert dates were something that took on mythical importance, and he was glad to be going with some of his best friends. I was the only dad among Evan's friends who would take them to the concerts, since the local dads wouldn't dream of sitting through such "loud noise." Well, I did, and now I am so glad that I got to make some of Evan's dreams come true.

Concerts these days are a frightening experience if you have the general admission tickets that put you on the arena floor. Evan was younger than most who attended the concerts, but he *really* wanted to go, so I took him. I attended the original Woodstock festival, so I have somewhat of a feel for concerts, but today's concerts are about much more than just the music. The excited, scared feeling of becoming part of the ever-expanding mosh pit was both alluring and frightening. It was like some primitive tribal ritual that Evan needed to go through in order to pass to manhood. Although the music was way too loud, even for me, I understood his need to be part of the music scene.

Evan danced and sang at the concerts, which was thrilling to see. He could totally let go, which he couldn't do at home or with his friends. At thirteen it wasn't cool to dance around wildly, but when thousands of other people were doing the same thing, it was okay. I remember fondly the sweating, happy young man who greeted me at the end of each event.

At his last concert, his favorite band was playing and I took Evan and some of his friends the day after seventh grade ended. I lost track of Evan, and got a little worried about him, after all there were about 10,000 kids in the auditorium, mostly wearing black, as was Evan. Fifteen minutes after the end of the concert, I spotted him with the biggest smile I had ever seen on his face. He said he moved to the front row of the auditorium right in front of the band. The guitar player, whom he really admired— (nicknamed "Dime Bag") had spit beer on him and threw his guitar pick at Evan, which stuck to his chest. Evan was shirtless at this point, thus giving the guitar pick the ability to stick to his beer soaked chest.

Once Evan got home he immediately took the stub from the concert and the guitar pick and put them together in a frame, along with all the other stubs from the concerts he attended. It was a magnificent night, and Evan's extreme happiness warmed my heart. I will remember his smile that night for the rest of my life. I'm so glad I took him. You can't possibly understand how glad.

A note received in November, 2001:

> *"I went to that Slipknot concert last week. It was good but I really wished Evan was there. He would have loved it. Me and a few of my friends that knew him dedicated a mosh pit to him. I kinda felt like he was there with me."*

I realized how much concerts meant to Evan and I knew that there were kids who really wanted to go but couldn't, because their parents won't take them. I have decided in the memory of my son to start taking kids to concerts so they can enjoy this wonderful experience as Evan did. In November of 2001 I took one of Evan's friends, a fellow guitar player who had never been to a concert, to the concert he had really wanted to go to. I told him to ask his parents and they said it was okay for me to take him.

When his parents showed up on the night of the concert to drop him off, they thanked me for taking their son and mentioned that this would be his first and last concert. It made me really sad for him. The concert was great for Evan's friend, and it was a mixture of extreme sadness and some joy for me, knowing that someone else was able to have his wish fulfilled, at least this one time.

I took another one of Evan friends to a Christmas Bash concert (2001) that featured some of Evan's favorite bands, which was also bittersweet for me. Providing these experiences is something that I am really committed to doing, and I will continue to take kids to concerts who have never gone, until I can't take it anymore. Then I hope someone will take my place. Perhaps thousands of parents could take my place! That would be nice. Concerts really meant a lot to Evan, which means that they meant a lot to me. One of the things I can do as a dad is to provide my children with various opportunities that are just for their pure enjoyment, not mine. It is typically those experiences that will live on in their memories.

I'm sure there are other events that would mean just as much to other children as rock concerts did to Evan. It is my sincerest hope that parents will take their kids to those events and let them have their chance to live their lives and do the things that they want to do, even though it may not be something that we as parents would enjoy. That isn't really the point.

Evan's guitar work took on a new level of importance over the summer. He was asked to join one band, but quit because the music wasn't heavy enough. He stayed on as their music advisor for a while, and was in the midst of getting another band together with a really good drummer and singer. He was quite excited about the possibility of playing the music he wanted to play with equally good musicians.

Evan somehow knew just what needed to be done to prepare for his role as lead guitarist. His computer was worked overtime as he downloaded many TAB instructions and learned new songs over the summer. Evan played a medley of Metallica songs that was simply incredible. I was amazed that at 13 he had such command of the guitar and put so much feeling into the music. He loved playing his guitar, and I was awed at his competence and dedication. He too, was awed at his own ability and delighted in playing metal music with his beloved Les Paul guitar.

> *"I think that everybody knew a different Evan. When I think of him, I remember the always kind, compassionate headbanger. When it comes to playing the guitar, nobody had a larger drive to better his skills than Evdogg (Evdogg was the nickname I gave him after he gave me the nickname Bawbdogg). I was always astounded that he had the dedication and patience to sit down for four hours just to learn a new technique. He would always tell me that I was the one who taught him to play; when I know that in reality it was those hours of working on a single technique that taught him to play. It seems that, when he had his Les Paul in hand, he had found his release from his responsibilities. He had a fathomless imagination, and I think that it manifested through his guitar playing. He had a profound love for guitar, and music in general.*
>
> *I will always remember Evdogg as one of my dearest friends. I will continue to admire his love for his family, and friends, his guitar talent and love for the instrument, and his profound love for heavy metal. I will never forget him, and I will count myself lucky for being able to say I truly knew him."*
> *— 17 year old neighbor, and an awesome guitar player who owns 8 guitars!)*

In the car Evan and I had a ritual. I would play Jimi Hendrix songs for Evan, as Jimi is my all time favorite musician. He would sort of listen to one song, and then it was his turn to play his favorite bands for me, hoping I would somehow convert. Neither one of us converted the other, but the music flowed back and forth, and it was loud and it was great. We both loved music, just different kinds. This past summer he said several times that he wanted to learn how to play classical guitar in order to help his finger picking, but I think secretly he admired the inspired and passionate style of some of the really good classical guitarists we used to listen to. I think, given the time, Evan would have developed his own style of music, and whatever that turned out to be, it would have been from his heart and most excellent.

"One of my best memories with Evan is a phone call we had. He sat in his room trying to remember how to play a song on guitar while I talked. Every time he'd be off by just one or two notes. After trying the song 5 or 6 times he finally got it. Even though we were just on the phone, I could tell that he was smiling and so proud of himself. He knew how talented he was and that he could conquer anything if he kept at it."
— a friend

Evan penned this ode to his Guitar as a seventh grade English project.

The Guitar
By Evan Holofcener

It was beautiful. It glowed with a warm cinnamon and faded like a sunset into a dark brown. All twenty-two frets shined like newly polished silver. The headset was beautifully handcrafted and hand carved into a work of art. It sounded like heaven if heaven were to have a sound. The mellow oak tones were always followed with a sharp bite from the mahogany finish. It was the most magnificent thing in the world. Yes, it was beautiful.

I spend every spare second on that guitar. Whenever I feel sad, I play guitar. Whenever I am happy, I play guitar. When I play I can let go of everything that holds me down. Any troubles at all are forgotten the second I pick up my guitar. All my feelings seem to flow out of me and into my music. My music is how I deal with my problems. My guitar is my whole life.

One day when I came into my room it was gone! It wasn't in its stand. It wasn't in its case either. My mind was racing. Where is it? Who took it? I hysterically searched the house. I looked in every nook and cranny yet there was no sign of my guitar. I galloped down the stairs and bombarded my mother with questions. She had no idea where it was.

> *I was now starting to lose it. I have put my whole life into that guitar. What will I do? I have spent hours upon hours on that guitar. My every spare second was spent on that guitar and now it's gone. My dream was to become rich and famous as a rock star. You can't become a rock star without a guitar! I must find my guitar.*
>
> *I was just about to call the police about my guitar when my father arrived home. I dashed out to the driveway screaming.*
>
> *"Where's my guitar?" I screamed.*
>
> *"I've got a little surprise for you," he said musically.*
>
> *He opened the trunk of the trunk of our car, and there it was. He had taken it to the shop to get it polished and tuned up. I snatched it into my hands and ran to my room. I plugged into my amp and screamed out the most amazing solo I had ever played.*

I'm keeping his Gibson Les Paul 1960 Classic guitar. I will never sell it. I polish it often as Evan did. Maybe it will come to good use one day besides a reminder of what was.

For some reason that is beyond my ability to completely understand, I cannot listen to any music, even on the radio in the car. That really hurts me because I love music and now I can't listen to it. I guess because Evan was so associated in my mind with music that I cannot bear to hear music without him. When I think of music playing, I think of Evan, which is too painful for me at this point. Thank goodness for National Public Radio (talk radio), the only program I can tolerate. The same phenomenon is also affecting Nancy as well.

Last three months-
A new feeling of power

February 2

It was in his last three months that the passion really kicked in. You could see it in Evan's weight loss program and just about everything else that he did. While he was losing pounds this past summer, he cut out all sugar and anything else he decided wasn't good for him. His fascination with his own body and how he could change it and sculpt it with daily weight training and exercise was interesting to observe. His dedication to anything he tried became obvious—-obvious in that he achieved everything he set out to do. He did what he wanted to do. While others may have wanted to do things, Evan did them.

> *"Evan was able to touch the lives of everyone he met. Not many people can do that. He was good at everything, and in the last three months of his life he was almost Godly with everything he did. He just got better and better. Evan had the right mind set to do and accomplish it 10x faster than anyone else. I will miss him more than words can express. His death has left a hole in me that I don't think anything can fill."*
> *— a friend*

Evan was definitely in a very heightened state of being the last few months, and I think it was as evident to Evan as well as those watching him in amazement. Something was happening that was accelerating at a very fast pace, and it was both unusual and fascinating to observe. Evan was feeling a power that he made reference to numerous times. We simply dismissed it at the time, but with hindsight, we better understand his references to feeling that power, and can only imagine what he may have been going through and experiencing. I have never seen anything like it in my life.

We could see it in his bike riding. Passionate, long, strenuous bike rides. Further and further he went, delighting in exploring every new trail and street. His fascination for experiencing new things was voracious. He never wanted to take the same bike ride twice and he didn't!. That would be too boring, too conventional. He was plotting to ride every trail in Groton (there are miles and miles of trails here) and his goal was to map out each and every trail and ride it. If Evan and I were riding, he would want to take a new route every time, and often decide to explore some trail that was new and enticing to him. I preferred the traditional routes, but would usually come over to his way of thinking, even though I have never been that adventurous.

"Evan and I took several hikes together since it was a good opportunity to chat about things but as a side light to the great scenic beauty that surrounded us. As soon as Evan and I dropped off Nancy and Ryan for a horse ride, we headed up a steep road to Yankee Boy Basin, a road that would have sent my sister into gripping the armrests. Evan simply looked out over the cliff next to the roadway and said 'how far do you think it is to the waterfall down there?' 'This is great', I said. I knew that I had a climbing partner who would enjoy the heights and depths that I so loved. Immediately I began making plans for other climbs, as we were like multiple reflections in mirrors held up to one another. Just as my boys had graduated to their own worlds of college and girlfriends, another climber had just announced himself.

Evan was one of the calmest, most contented kids I have known. He was just enjoying the moment, and talked casually about his life, his girlfriend Elizabethe, nutrition and how he was building himself up for the hockey season by exercising. I sensed that he had put the dark stuff behind him and had worked out a new pathway that allowed him a new measure of freedom, something very advanced for his age. Something that made him at ease with himself and very peaceful.

I think Evan had the most collected, calm, peaceful and joyful life that anyone could hope for. That's the image I carry forth every day: a happy youth now on his next great adventure. He's just getting there before me. I'm sad that he won't be with me on all of those hikes I had in mind, but I have the feeling that the next time we meet, he'll show me some astounding summits that he'll have already mastered. I have a lot to practice for...."

Uncle Ken on Evan's trip to Colorado Summer of 2001.

Ken is an accomplished mountain climber having climbed all 54 14,000-foot mountains in Colorado.

Evan was always looking for the new adventure, the new experience, something that would allow him the freedom of discovering something on his own. He loved to discover things; it made him feel good, and it was consistent with his striving nature. Never do the boring thing; never do the traditional thing that others can easily do. He wanted to be the first one to try something new.

Evan had a daily regimen during last summer that consisted of getting up, making protein shakes, going online with his friends, going for a bike ride, working on our weight machine while talking on the phone with friends, watching "Saturday Night Live" reruns or Comedy Central, going online, playing guitar, downloading songs for his guitar, going on another bike ride, played more guitar, more shakes, maybe enjoying an evening meal, watching MTV. Then, in the evening, he would sometimes put on his roller blades and blade around the neighborhood, often doing 10 miles in total darkness with only a flashlight to guide him.

Another change for Evan over the summer concerned his thoughts about the future. He finally had the realization that he had to get serious about making his dreams come true and started plotting his course. He knew he had to get good grades, since he wanted to go to a good college. Evan was excited about his future. It was all going to be so good. He knew he could make his dreams come true. He just knew it!

Evan definitely wanted to be a famous rock star, which was certainly in the realm of possibilities. The most recent memory I have thought is that he wanted to be a counselor and help troubled kids, something he was already doing to some extent. I think he would have continued to make a difference in the lives of many kids, and hopefully he still can.

"We all miss him so much, and his bright spirit will continue to make a difference in the lives of those who knew and loved him, like us. I am so glad my daughter had him in her life. I am so glad we all did. We will always remember him and let his bright spirit continue to make a difference in our lives."
— a neighborhood mom

The week before eighth grade started, he cleaned his room, his closets, and his drawers, and took an inventory of his clothes. His mom couldn't believe it and didn't understand the inventory. He said that he had so many clothes, but that they were really "scrubby," and it looked like he had more clothes that he actually did, so that when we went shopping for school clothes, he could figure out what he needed.

He spent hours getting his folders and book dividers ready for school, emblazoned with his favorite band pictures. After finding out that he was on the same school team as Elizabethe, he was so happy. His hockey coach was the same one as last year, and that was the icing on the cake. The kids spent hours on line, trying to find out who was on which team at school. Evan organized a list of team members and emailed it to the 150+ people on his AOL IM list.

Evan told some of his friends just before school started that his life was perfect. He had finally pulled it together, set goals for himself, and found that with hard work he could achieve anything. Evan had even made a conscious effort to get along better with his brother and showered him with affection that last week, showing Ryan how to gel his hair and dress the cool way for the coming school year. Ryan loved it, as did Evan.

February 13

Ryan wanted to be included in this book and the interview format worked best because it enabled him to get out his feelings in the way that he wanted them to be expressed.

Interview with Ryan Maxwell Holofcener. After Evan's death, we gave Ryan Evan's middle name, Maxwell, which he was proud to have.

How do you feel now about Evan's death?

Really sad and just missing him all the time. Feeling unsafe because he used to protect me when anybody used to pick on me, even though I could handle it myself, he would still be there to protect me.

What have you learned since the accident?

I noticed that people still, after Evan's accident aren't wearing bike helmets, and an inch of Styrofoam could save someone's life anywhere.

What advice would you give to people who have lost a brother?

It's okay to cry because that's what I didn't do, and just let yourself go free. If you start to cry you should get some water to calm yourself and spend time with people so you don't get lonely. That's what our family did for Christmas and Thanksgiving.

How does it feel not having Evan around?

Feels really bad and boring cause we always used to fight and play sports. We were just starting to get along really, really well. It's really sad because he just isn't around anymore and just a simple accident could be fatal.

If you could talk to Evan now and you knew he was listening what would you say?

I would try to comfort him about being dead. And tell him about all we did at the ceremonies like the hockey jersey ceremony, and everybody really, really misses you and we are all very sad to have you go. We also had a memorial service for you and you don't know how many people came over, it was way over a hundred. We got a new puppy and she is really cute and her name is Chloe. We went up to Michigan for Christmas and had a really good time but I wish you were there.

What is the point of living?

Why do we just get born to die another day? The answer is that it is to make accomplishments and make people happy for who they are and what they are.

February 18

At the end, Evan had the ability to figure out everything. I have never seen anything like it. He could literally do anything. Nothing was impossible for him. He seemed to have an inner knowledge of how things operated, including people. He could repair everything at our house. I asked him once to fix our automatic garage door, as it wasn't opening properly. I knew that he had never fixed an automatic garage door before. Evan just did it. He didn't stop to think he couldn't. He just figured it out. Everything was easy for him at the end. EVERYTHING!

I was too enthralled with my own self demise to realize that I can be truly happy, that life really is worth living. Evan found the joy in all that he did. He had the power to help, and heal anyone who needed it. Sometimes people didn't even ask, he just knew. He "just knew" a lot of things, and people trusted him, more than they would trust any other soul. For a lot of people Evan brought "true happiness," if so, would it or could it be like Evan? I hope someday to have the answers to these questions, until then I

search and search, and search. Thank you SO much for setting me in the right direction."
— a friend who read a rough draft of this book.

February 20

Going in Evan's room after his death was unnerving. It was so clean and devoid of anything non-essential. He had his guitars of course, as well as various trophies that he wanted to put in the attic because they didn't mean anything to him anymore. He also had a small collection of books, all of which were of the "Life strategies for Teens" variety.

All his life his room had been messy, filled with lots of clutter and junk. That last week he thoroughly cleaned his room getting ready for school. I wish that there were more things to look through and discover. With his stark black walls, the feeling was eerie, and unsettling. It makes me sad that there was so little to discover in his room. I was hoping to find treasure troves of secret letters, hidden music tapes, and unfound poems. I wanted to spend time reading and re-reading them over and over. There was nothing hidden, except for a few old girlfriend letters. I wanted more Evan, and I couldn't get it.

After Evan's death, we received many wonderful letters and cards and emails, from friends, and from parents of friends, telling us about their impressions of, and time spent with Evan. It was soothing to receive all of the information and experiences with Evan, and Nancy and I felt comforted in knowing that Evan had a happy life at the end, but also that he touched so many other lives during his short life. Although when I say short life, I am measuring it with time, not accomplishments. Accomplishments are a much more accurate measurement of one's life.

"When I met Elizabethe at your home in Groton, I could completely understand why you were crazy about her. She was awesome! I got to see your room for the first time (what were you thinking about when you put that hole through your door, just kidding). She and I talked about you and how funny you were and are. I still talk to her online today and when I go and visit your

parents I hope to see her.
Evan, you taught me so many things that are now so important in my life. You taught me to be more athletic, to take chances and risks, to face your fears, to not be afraid of what people think of you and to speak your mind. Without these lessons I could have never been the person that I am today. Our friendship filled my life with meaning and fun that I will never forget. I still think about you all the time and even dream about you. Right now I know you are in a good place and I miss you, but I know that I will see you at the end of my life where we will be able to hug each other again. I love and miss you Evan and I will always have a place for you in my heart."
—Evan's dear friend from Washington, D.C.

Evan was a wonderful son and a most excellent big brother. He was really fun and interesting to be with because he was so lively and had such an interesting view of life on just about any topic, and certainly wasn't shy about sharing his opinions. Evan was easy to be with and he delighted in being who he was. We delighted in being in his company, well most of the time anyway. Remember he was still a teenager.

I feel really sad that I will never have the pleasure of seeing how amazing Evan would have become in whatever chosen field he wanted to master. I think he would have made his indelible mark on the world of music and brought great joy to himself and others. If he followed through with his desire to be a therapist helping teenagers, I am positive he would have helped a lot of people. I will miss not seeing him get married and have children. He would have been a wonderful father. We often talked about his (future) children when we went on our bike rides together. Evan talked about his kids and how he would take them on bike rides hoping to instill in them his love of biking. He wanted his kids to love all the things he did, in the way that he did. Those kids would have had a wonderful father and teacher and friend in Evan. He never wanted his kids to watch TV, which I thought was interesting. He was sure of one thing: his kids would be really cool, just like him. I have no doubt they would have turned out that way.

Since Evan's goals were so high and he put so much pressure on himself to always do his best, life for Evan would have always been a struggle, which requires a constant ongoing effort. His life would have been good I am sure, but not easy, because his chosen path was difficult. Only climbers who wanted to conquer the highest mountains are on the same path Evan was on. The climb, which would have lasted his entire life, would have been challenging, but worth it. Evan would have never given up when things got tough and he would have planted his EH flag on the top of the highest peak there is.

This journal is about a child who had the proper background for success but realized it was really up to him to make it happen.. He *"did* make it happen by using the skills he had and developed: the ones he needed to face this world with courage, passion, conviction, and dedication. We can all be better than we are. We only need to put into motion the things we know we should do. Evan did what he needed to do in order to have the life that he desired to have. It is the actions put into place that transformed Evan's life into something incredible and wonderful. We all have the same potential. It's just a question of applying the knowledge of what we must do and DO IT!

I am so glad Evan never put off *living* his life until tomorrow. He never knew his tomorrows were going to be so few. And neither do any of us!

> *"I think about all that he had accomplished in thirteen years here and I continue to realize that I must look to my own son for inspiration in my life. There was one special moment we had together when the IMing was slow and I sat down to talk to him. I had been thinking about all he had accomplished and wanted to acknowledge his success. I told him about Alfred Adler and how he theorized what made a person a successful human being.*
>
> *There are four areas that we seek accomplishment in; finding the right life's work to become a contributing member of our society; finding the right social group or "family" he fit into; having a connection to his spirit which was very strong and being able to find someone to love and love him back (the ability to achieve intimacy with someone).*

I told him that I had been thinking about his hard work so far and realized that he would be considered a successful human being at the age of thirteen! Some people spend their whole lives and never find the right person or the deep sense of self he had developed. Some people never figure out what they are supposed to do and help others while doing it. He looked at me and smiled shyly and said "oh yeah?"

I have no doubt that he would have been successful because his sense of self and his ability to commit was so strong. I've never known anyone so careful to choose the right path for himself because in reality I think he realized that this life was an incredible thing to play with and mold into whatever he had the power to.

So now in my life, I look to my son's life and hope that some of his determination, fearlessness and caring for his friends can rub off on me somehow. I thought that it was my job as a parent to teach him everything he needed to know to go out into the world and make it on his own. Seems that the lessons I learned from him are still being realized. I feel his life and passing taught me the thing I was put here on earth for. This unfolds and surprises me daily at the depth of love and aching."

— Mom

Observations

March 5

This tragedy has not only changed my life and the lives of Nancy and Ryan, it also changed the lives of his friends, our neighbors, and families of children that never knew him, but knew of him. There are many things that I can see now that I couldn't see before, and my earlier realizations about life and the meaning of life are greatly enhanced and accelerated. I need to share my updated view of life and the observations that come easily to me now. This is the kind of information I wish I had earlier in my own life, as it would have helped me to start thinking about life in a way that had never been presented to me. I also wish I could have shared my new vision with Evan at the beginning of his own earthly journey.

For many years, I have tried to find the meaning in life, not wanting to take other peoples' beliefs and concepts and adapt them as my own, although I certainly had my share of beliefs nonetheless. Belief in something is not knowing it, otherwise we would say we knew or know. Belief is a hope that what we believe is true. That's it, just a hope, because we don't and can't really know if a belief is true.

If we aren't positive about something, we say we believe it is true. We are positive about something by experiencing it via our five senses, thus making it real. Belief versus knowing is vastly different. Do we say "I believe I love you," or do we say "I love you" when we love someone? Two very different meanings. It is possible to move from belief to knowing by having an inner experience that lets us remove the doubt we may have been feeling and *know*.

Well meaning people at the funeral service for Evan had so many things to say about him. *"Evan is in a much better place now.*" How do they know? *"Evan is in heaven.*" How can they say that? Do they have some inside contact in heaven who said, *"hey Evan's here*?" I don't think so.

I started thinking about the randomness of how we choose the words that comfort us in times of grief. It really does seem like such an arbitrary process. Okay. Evan is in a better place. All right, I'll believe that. Why? Because it makes me feel better. In many ways there is certainly no logic to it. Actually, we can believe anything that we want to, thus making that belief true and "real," to us. To me, that's the really scary part, since I can believe anything I want to, and *that* is where I find my solace, and my comfort? I think if we were to look at this process with a critical eye it couldn't make sense, but we don't analyze our beliefs, as they comfort us, and that seems to be enough for most people.

Somehow, all of the ideas and concepts I had from over 30 years of delving into the religious and spiritual realms left me, up until September 1, 2001, with a plethora of things to say to people about everything and anything. However, after Evan's death, I knew nothing, nothing at all. I didn't and couldn't understand what happened to Evan, where he was, and most importantly, why he had to die. Why? That is the real destroyer. You cannot understand why. No one on this earth can actually tell me why— what happened to Evan— occurred. Of course there are probably lots of people who have their ideas, but to me, the exploration of why is like the Tower of Babel: it's easy for people to offer us their opinions, as their ideas seem so interesting and fascinating to them.

Our beliefs are the backup systems we have adopted to help us in times of need. Basically, they comfort us when something goes wrong according to our own plans about how we believe this life should be, although we might not think of our own beliefs in this way. I don't really think many of us take the time to think about our beliefs at all. Since most of us don't have tragic situations in our lives, we don't have the need to call upon them to help us in times of trouble, and I'm not simply talking about the loss of a job or not getting good grades in school. In many ways, our beliefs are like a data storage backup system that has never been tested, since most of us have never experienced a real tragedy that we needed to call up our belief system in order to comfort us.

If we have never experienced a great loss we cannot know if our beliefs will in fact comfort us when the time comes. We cannot simply imagine a tragedy and put our beliefs into play, like a simulation of something awful. It doesn't work that way

In some ways, our beliefs may actually keep us from knowing more about this life. Simply having a belief will prevent some of us from looking deeper into the meaning and purpose of life, because we think that our belief is the ultimate answer. What if it isn't? We won't really know if our belief was sufficient in magnitude to believe in until we are dead, and then we still might not know. If we were wrong it will be our tough luck and too late to change anything. If our beliefs are soothing enough that we aren't searching, we may not get to where we need to go, in terms of real understanding. After all we cannot find the truths about this life until and unless we are actively searching for them. I am not saying, that having beliefs are bad, because they aren't. It's just that we should put them in their proper perspective, and that will be different for each individual.

If you have the same belief system that was handed down to you from your parents, you may want to validate your searching and make sure that your belief is something that *you* have come up with after researching various alternatives. We should certainly feel that our beliefs were formed by intelligent thinking, rather than handed down to us from generation to generation, like used furniture.

It would be interesting to write down your beliefs, as many as possible, and really look at them to see if your beliefs can stand up to your own critical analysis. This would be an interesting exercise to do within a family at a family meeting. I think the results would surprise you.

After intensive searching for answers following Evan's death, I do have a few beliefs that are comforting to me and I am glad I have them, because they make me feel better about Evan and his time here on earth. After all my talking about beliefs versus knowledge, I now, with some time passed from September 1st, find that if you have beliefs and feel good about them, then they are in fact helpful, and I am grateful for the comfort they provide. The investigation into my own beliefs was a healing process and one that I am glad, upon reflection that I went through. Of course I would have preferred the circumstance to have been different that caused my introspection in the first place.

Still, I would rather know one thing rather than have 1,000 beliefs.

"Where am I? Caught in intricacies that I will never be able to understand, because what I want to be challenged by is what will happen to me after death. I find that challenging. Why? Because I am so unsure about now. That's why I wonder what's going to happen to me when I'm gone. When you're sure about now, it's not like that. When I am uncertain of where I am, I am uncertain of everything. When I am certain of where I am, it's okay. It really is." Maharaji, July 1, 2001

I did try to read some of the self-help books about loss, but they didn't help. So many ideas, so many opinions, so many people believing that they have the right answer. Good intentioned as they were however, my spirit was still deeply wounded and I couldn't find any relief. To me those books were just more words describing water, when I was dying of thirst. I wanted water, not thoughts or ideas about water. I couldn't be comforted without being helped to find the meaning of my Evan's brief life on earth, without words. I needed to know that his life had a reason—that there was a purpose in his being alive and departing so suddenly. Otherwise, what's the point? What impact did he have on this world? Did he actually have an impact? Was he meant to have an impact? It doesn't make sense that a life so bright and so promising would end this way, and at this time.

Was God to blame? I don't think so. God isn't a person. Where did that idea start? God is energy and can be experienced within each one of us. That is my experience, not a theory. We don't need to have ideas about our Creator, as we were meant, from the beginning, to have an *experience* that lets us see what is and what isn't real. Do you really think that knowledge about God would be left to scholars and religious figures? It can't be that way; it just can't.

God doesn't pick on people and cause them suffering while rewarding others that seemingly have the "good life." How do I know that? I have realized it within myself. This isn't a philosophy, at least for me. You can believe anything you want to. What we believe doesn't change anything or make something right, just because we believe it.

It's not possible that God would discriminate against any of its creations. Otherwise nothing would make sense. Why are some people "blessed," and others are "cursed?" Reading many spiritual books by authors who have been involved in working with people that had near death experiences like Dr. Elizabeth-Kübler Ross or past life regressionists, like Dr. Brian Weiss are basically saying the same thing: that we essentially pick our situations or earth to have the maximum learning capabilities. You don't have to either believe or disbelieve this statement. Whether we learn or not from our situations in life is really up to us. Yet not everyone learns their lessons, even though things are set up optimally for that purpose. Some lessons are really hard, but we don't have any choice over the things that happen in our lives. If we did, nothing bad would ever happen to anyone on the planet, but that isn't the case is it?

I can't bring Evan back. It's up to me to understand the lessons that I need to learn from this experience. I now ask myself the question *"what can I learn from this situation?"* when bad things happen. If something has already happened, we can't change it, but we can learn from it. While this may sound cold, to me the pain and suffering from Evan's death is quite real, and something that I experience every single day. However, I must continue with my life and uncover what I can about my purpose on this earth and try and go forward with my own earthly education.

Nancy and I have been attending Compassionate Friends (group for parents who have lost children) meetings to provide us with some sense of perspective, by being with other parents who have lost a child. There are parents there who have done their best to move forward, and there are there are those who cannot move on because the guilt or the pain is too much for them to bear. Being happy again, even briefly, seems to mock the memory of their departed child. Two sets of parents with the same loss looking at life so differently, and either learning to go forward to fulfill their own lives and seek a sense of wholeness, or stuck in the past, with the almost unbearable pain from the early departure of their child. Which would you choose? It is a choice. We all have choices in life, whether to move forward, regardless of how hard things are, or choose to be stuck in our pain, not moving forward and not moving backward. Stuck in time, stuck in pain, stuck in our wanting to do something to take the pain away, but not doing it. We cannot change the past, but we can change our future, to some extent.

I think it is easier to face the pain and move on, but thinking about facing the pain is too painful for some people. They retreat into their defensive mode, not realizing that the breakthrough they imagine would be so painful is actually so much less painful than being immobilized. Choosing to face the pain is the way to break through. There isn't another way, although it is still a choice.

March 19

The senselessness of Evan's death seemed to surface a belief that I thought had vanished along with all the others: he was at the wrong place at the wrong time, even down to the wrong second, as one second either way would have saved him. The road Evan was biking on is a rural country road with very little traffic even on a normal day, and it was a holiday weekend, when many local people generally go to the mountains or the beach. The population in Groton is only 9,900. There isn't one traffic light or parking meter in our town, and people who live here like it that way.

The part of the road where the accident occurred is straight, and Evan and the driver of the pick-up truck that hit him could see each other for at least a half mile. Evan was riding on the sidewalk (as he always did when not riding on the trials), which was facing oncoming traffic. He was hit where the road curved at a five degree angle, according to the police. The driver kept on going straight and Evan just happened to be at the exact spot where the road starts to curve at the exact time the driver was leaving the road. The driver then went up onto the sidewalk, heading toward the woods, again according to the police. The odds of

Evan being at that spot with a car going off the road, at exactly the same place, at the exact same time, has to be quite high. It makes me wonder about one of my old beliefs. If it is your time to go, you are going to go, and you will be at the wrong place at the wrong time, or the right place at the right time, according to your destiny.

Is there order in the universe, or is everything just a bunch of random occurrences, something that I find hard to accept? It can't be part order and part chaos, can it? Either there is order in the universe, or there isn't. So I guess I do have a few beliefs left, because I don't know if it's true, but somehow I do believe in the order of things and I can't imagine it any other way, although that still doesn't make me feel better.

March 21

After Evan's death something changed in me. I was looking out at the world through a whole new perspective. Something inside me opened up—something that I cannot express or explain changed. There was almost an instantaneous shift in my consciousness that was quite noticeable to me, and probably to the people who know me well. I have changed, and changed for the better. Consciousness, when we get more in touch with it, however that happens, is always good. It is a direct link to our higher self, which is our better self. It is us as we could or should be.

When hearts and minds are opened, even for a brief moment, something wonderful can happen if we just give it a chance. Sometimes, we can't control when and if that event occurs. Typically it is when something awful happens in our life. Then we are looking for help from God. When we seek something, that's typically when we find it, perhaps not what we were asking for but what we needed.

Evan's untimely death started a reaction that in a sense accelerated my own evolution. I can't explain it better than that. When we are put in touch with our higher consciousness, it's as if a reset button has been pushed, reverting us back to the manufacturer's original specs. The way we were meant to be. That's the way I feel now.

When that reset button is pushed, life becomes much simpler. It is very clear what is important and what isn't. Most of the stuff that we think is important isn't, and of course the reverse is true. Material things are less important, promotions and jobs are less important, status is less important. It doesn't mean that those things aren't important—just less so. Family, friends, helping others, doing the right things (you know what they are), are much more important. Love is very important. Feeling at one with ourselves is more important. God is more important, not in a religious sense, but in a spiritual sense.

The mirror that I look into now to see if my life is on track is clear, no longer covered by a foggy mist, making it easier to see the mistakes I've made, and the things that I am doing right. We can only judge what is right or wrong for ourselves. No one else can do that, even though they may try. For those who look and see the pain of things not done, or wrongly done, it's not so bad. First we have to have the "sight" to be able to see the things in our lives that need changing, and then change them. This is easier said than done. It's actually the hardest thing in our life that we have to do, and it does involve a lot of effort— not just a one time effort either.

> *"So, I look at if from the perspective that concerns me. And what is that perspective? It is simple. I have a lot of seconds, and a few less minutes than seconds. Fewer yet are the hours, fewer than that are the days and fewer than that are the weeks. Fewer than that, the months come, fewer than that, the years, and fewer than that the decades. But fewer even than that, a lifetime. Only one. The seconds and minutes can't be counted on your fingers-there would be too many. When it comes to decades, you can at least start counting them on your two hands. But when it comes to your lifetime, all you need is one finger.*
>
> *One lifetime—that is all I have. One existence—this is what I have. And unless I comprehend that, how can I shape my future, and what can I learn from my past.*
>
> *If I want to be fulfilled, then I need to realize that every moment that I haven't been fulfilled is a moment that has been wasted.*

And every moment that will come to me brings with it the possibility either of me being fulfilled, or the moment being wasted."

— Maharaji

Seeing what must be done and doing it is vastly different. It's similar to having a cut. If we take care of it right away, it will heal; but if we are too busy to take care of it or are afraid the cure will hurt, we are simply postponing the inevitable. It must be dealt with at some time or another. If the procrastination is severe, the cut will become infected and *"now* the cure will be far more painful, and the suffering increased. You cannot put things off in hope that they will go away. They won't. By not looking at the problems in your life and the causes of the problems, the problems will never get resolved, and the resultant pain from unresolved issues is avoidable. Our unresolved issues will always be there waiting for us, hiding, festering inside of us, waiting for resolution.

It sounds like so many things involve pain, but the suffering we are going through is avoidable for the most part. That is not to say sadness is avoidable, or unhappiness is avoidable. To some degree they are, depending on our actions to resolve the issues that are troubling us, and those are the issues that need the resolution. And of course, our perspective can allow us to face things with a "second sight" that will enable us to face life differently, much more open to the way things *really* are.

My perspective on all of this is no doubt quite different from most other people. I have been thrust into an alternate perspective, which permits me to see things I was previously unable to see. My perspective was as yours may be now. I feel as if I am reporting from sometime or place in the future, and I hope that you can feel what it is I am trying to convey. If there is one thing I have learned from Evan's death it is that I understand what I need to do for the rest of my life.

It is my nature at this point to look at everything critically, and I don't accept anything at face value, because I know there is much more, or much less to everything that exists. So when I have an understanding of something at this point, it has already gone through a very thorough process of trying to be rejected, but if it is delivered in a special way, then I am more open to the information. Sorry if this sounds confusing, but it is confusing even to me, because my understanding of this life is being given to me as a wonderful gift meant to share, and that is what I am doing.

Oftentimes, I think the wisest people on this planet are those who have undergone the most suffering. They know what is important and what isn't. If you can't get the message that is trying to be conveyed through this book, find someone who is in real pain, someone who has lost a child or a friend, or who has suffered great tragedy, and tell them your problems. Your problems will be put in their proper perspective in a nano-second, if the person is honest with you. It is important to try and not intellectually understand the message contained in this book, but to somehow feel it. Understanding of the basic truths about our life on earth is not meant only for the intellectually gifted.

> *"What about that lamp within that needs to be lit? What about this voice that needs to be heard? The world demands much of me. I must be a father. I must be a friend. I must do this, I must do that. But what about me? What about this life? What about that lamp within that needs to be heard? A voice that doesn't have big requests; all it says is, "Be content." There is no greater company than Truth. You won't find it written on a piece of paper. Truth comes from within. It is unaltered, unchanged, and has been here as long as human beings have walked on this earth."*
>
> *— Maharaji June 16, 1997 England*

Many people have experienced understanding or developed theories about life and our earthly journey, but some of them remind me of the parable about the blind men "seeing" an elephant: one felt the tail, another felt the trunk, another felt the legs, and yet another felt the belly. The four blind men all got together to compare notes, and began arguing about what an elephant was. The man who felt the tail compared the elephant to a rope, and each of them described the elephant from his single perspective. Since we know each man only felt a part of the elephant, it was not possible for them to have a common experience. Similarly, it is that way with theories about this life. Some people see only their part of the overall picture. The whole picture however, is a composition of all the parts.

It all has to do with the pain level we are experiencing in our lives. If things are going well, we don't search for *the answers* or most likely any answers. Why should we? There isn't an urgent need to find something if we are content with our life. On the other hand, if we are suffering, either physically or mentally, we are much more active in looking for answers for our questions. Why me? What is going on here? How can I find this elusive thing called happiness?

Some people that aren't suffering are looking for answers; and many seemed to have found the answers through their religion, and will defend their beliefs vigorously when confronted about the purpose of this life. But remember, we can believe anything we want to, so how solid are those beliefs if we can in fact choose any one we want, or feel comfortable with?

What would happen to your religious beliefs if you somehow woke up in a state of complete forgetfulness, and couldn't remember anything about your past and had no one that you knew to give you information about your life. What would your religion be then? How would you choose your religion, with no past impressions given to you and no one to tell you what you were to believe in?

If we weren't burdened with a preconception of what to believe, what would we believe? If religion was important to you, how would you find a religion that you would be comfortable with starting from scratch? How would you go about it? How would you know which one to believe in when they all say that their version of God is the only way? Interesting question, isn't it?

My Father

March 28

My father always lived his life according to his own desires, never pondering the spiritual realms that would perhaps have given him a different perspective on life. I once read that Jeffrey Dahmer, the serial killer, felt free to commit his ghastly murders because he didn't believe in God or heaven and hell so he thought it didn't make any difference what he did. Our beliefs do, in many ways, lead us in certain directions, and influence the way we behave, depending on our commitment to our own beliefs.

My father was diagnosed with terminal cancer in December of 2001 and given a prognosis of three months to live. Upon the realization that his death was imminent one would think that this would be the time to right the wrongs in his life to the extent that he could. Hopefully he would be reflecting on his life and the fact that it was ending soon and what did it all mean, if anything? However, my Dad really didn't believe in anything beyond this life or God, and since he didn't believe in anything, in his mind it didn't make any difference what he did. This is really sad, and was probably the reason he has acted the way that he did in his life. Actually, he sort of had beliefs, but really didn't believe in his beliefs. Having no belief or faith in your beliefs is like having no beliefs at all.

I spent six days with him in January of 2002 watching him grow weaker and weaker, day by day. I have always had a difficult relationship with my dad. I went to see him to take care of unfinished business, as I needed to do "the right thing," by taking care of him and saying what I needed to say to him. I realized that when I left that I did what I should have and said what I should have, but still I had not taken care of what I needed to do, because I was insincere. The words I said had no feeling behind them. I thought that the actions themselves would be sufficient, but I realized they weren't.

A month later I went back. I did the right thing for the right reason, and felt wonderful taking really good care of him. It was definitely one of the hardest things I have ever done, but at the end of my visit, it felt great, because I had faced my unfinished business and found the fear and pain went away when confronted.

I now know that finally, I have taken care of all the unfinished business with my Dad. I saw him looking at me rather strangely, wondering how I could be so caring and thoughtful. I certainly didn't learn it from him, but in a way I did. I learned that the opposite of bad is good. I have learned my lessons well from watching a life that was spent taking care of no one but himself, with no spiritual connection. I was witnessing the sad conclusion. No friends to care about him, and only a few people in his life who wanted to visit with him while he was dying. And they were only hanging around hoping to get some money for their "friendship." A lonely unsatisfying conclusion to a life so filled with promise.

My Dad was starting to think about resolving some issues, as he actually discussed his need to, but his physical and mental capacity were preventing him from doing so. He could only think about resolving issues, and how painful that must have been; the thought that he made so many mistakes, and was unable to correct them because he waited too long. Two months earlier it would have been possible, but he only accepted the fact that he was dying in the last few weeks of his life, although he knew about his terminal condition for months. He literally couldn't do anything to change things, since he was too weak, but he was still consciousness enough to realize that he wanted to. That has to be painful.

In February, 2002 my Dad mentioned to his hospice nurse that he still wasn't ready to go. Can you imagine, 83 years old and he still wasn't ready to go? It boggles my mind that someone couldn't get it together to prepare for the inevitable given so much time. In reality it doesn't matter whether he was ready to go or not. When his time was up he was going to go, regardless of whether he was ready. And that's ultimately what happened. To think that he was able to be conscious of the finality of his life for at least 60 years and not to be ready is really sad and really pathetic. Since he never thought about the end, he never prepared for it. Dad never talked about death to me or anyone that I know.

I tried to steer the conversation towards death; about his expectations and beliefs when we were together after his terminal prognosis, thinking that it might be of some comfort having someone to listen to him He never dealt with it. Minutes before he died, at the end of February, he was trying to say something to Nancy. The words never came out. I wonder what he wanted to say?

Our choices in life will either bite us in the end or reward us. We don't get away with anything.

Happiness

March 30

I think one way to gauge how we are doing is to look at how happy we are, what it is that is making us happy, and what would happen if we suddenly lost those things or those people? Is our happiness hanging on a string, dependent on other people or situations that can be altered at any time? Most of us would have to admit it is, but if we are happy, we typically don't question anything, after all, we are happy, right?

What is happiness? This question is one of the most important questions that we can ever ask ourselves and each other. If we don't know what happiness is and how to obtain it, we will perhaps spend our lives in search of something that we might never find. Many people believe that happiness is making a lot of money, or being married, or having children, or getting the perfect job, or getting good grades in school, or being accepted into the right crowd, or traveling the world. For those people that have obtained "happiness" many reveal afterwards that what they obtained isn't as good as the scenario that was originally envisioned. The vision and the reality don't always match up.

If our happiness is dependent on anything other than ourselves, we will certainly be disappointed, because we cannot control people or situations. If our happiness is dependent on being married, what happens if we fall out of love, or our partner dies? What will happen to our happiness?

It's like having a sword hanging over our head that can fall at any time and destroy our happiness. Most of us are unaware that the sword even exists or that it is hanging by a thread so close to our proximity and can change our life instantaneously. That sword is called life. We know intellectually and statistically that situations can change, people can die. Realistically we think that those statistics apply to other people. Remember those other people think the same way.

We're thrilled when we get a new car, but the feeling wears off some months later. It's the same with so many things. The pursuit is much more exciting than the capture. The excitement wears off, and now the chasing looks more exciting, searching for the new, new thing, as someone recently called it.

Wouldn't it be wonderful to be able to give each child a handbook when they become teenagers, that would contain the secret to being happy? How many parents have had a heart to heart talk with their children about how to live a satisfied life? Probably not many, since the parents themselves have not obtained the satisfaction they were seeking and may be too embarrassed to have such a conversation with their kids, particularly if they would look foolish or ignorant. But, since the younger kids (pre-teen) wouldn't get it, and the older kids (teenagers) wouldn't listen, this task is almost impossible anyway.

Of course happiness is different things to different people. As all of the scriptures have indicated, happiness that is found within is the deepest and most pure. It couldn't be any other way, if we thought carefully about it.

In some ways, being happy is both dependent on ourselves and serving others. We cannot focus on ourselves to the exclusion of others and think that we will obtain the satisfaction one gains from helping other people. On the other hand, only helping other people cannot bring us the full inner happiness, which is the true source of satisfaction and fulfillment, and can only be found by going within.

I would like to share a hint with teenagers that will perhaps save them from searching for that "something" they will not be able to find in this world. Spirituality is the key: without it, you will spend your time in the pursuit of happiness that is not obtainable. This information is coming from my experience. Whether or not you believe what I have just suggested is true, I would hope that it is possible to focus on getting in touch with your spiritual nature. You will be able to see for yourself the difference in your life, as I have, and many, many others have as well.

I know that some of you will not really understand what I am trying to say until a tragedy actually does happen. That's the way it happened to me. That seems to be the way it works, as words such as these are just another set of beliefs with which you may either agree or disagree. I'm not sure how many of us even understand that there is a bigger picture, since our view is so limited. It's not really our fault; it's just the way it is. We don't even realize that our view is limited. How can we, unless we are somehow removed from our life and given a new perspective?

If one could obtain a new perspective without having to go through a tragedy, that would be wonderful, and could alleviate a lot of pain and suffering in our lives. The key is being open, and searching.

Success

March 31

Success is another matter, as there are so many misconceptions about the nature of success and who has obtained it. When we are just starting out in life, we think that we would like to be successful, without an understanding of how to be successful, or what constitutes success.

To some people, success is the big house, the important job, the right schools, and the exotic cars. Others believe that success is achieved if they are doing the things they want to do in life, although those things may not have brought them riches or fame. Still others, if they can be honest, would realize upon deep introspection that they are not and have never been successful, because their goals kept moving, never staying still long enough to provide the satisfaction a person should feel when they are successful.

Actually, is it success we are after or the perceived feeling that being successful would bring? Success can be looked upon as doing well at something, which is either felt by us or pronounced by others. But it is difficult for us to judge ourselves. Leaving the pronouncement whether or not we are successful to others is a process that is dependent on the person giving the pronouncement. Many people can only feel successful if their company or friends anoint them so, which is kind of sad, as success can be thought of as much more than doing well at work or being validated by friends.

It is within each one of us to be a successful father, mother, husband, wife, artist, healer, or being successful in many others aspects of our lives other than work. Many people still hold on to the perception that success is measured only by the jobs we have, or status in the community, or the amount of money we have. Success is more than that.

In *Leaders Magazine* published in April, 2002 Maharaji was asked about the meaning of success.

> *"If you don't feel successful within yourself it doesn't matter how successful you are on the outside. There is always going to be a distinction between the two. If you are the CEO of a big corporation, you have to come home, and what happens then? You may have a big office, a lot of power, but when you come home, you're just yourself. You need to be a success there, too. Once you draw the distinction between you and everything else, it's very easy to see that outward success is not what really matters."*

When I went to my twentieth high school reunion, I was thinking about my life and whether or not I had measured up to the ideal I had of myself at 20 years beyond high school. I experienced much success at work but I never became a millionaire, like some of my classmates. I was not famous as some in my graduation class were. However, I felt really successful. I looked around the room at all my old classmates and I had the feeling that I was successful in the truest sense of the word, because I found what I was looking for within me! I found the gift that was meant to be found. To this day, I feel like one of the luckiest people in the world, although I wish one event in my life didn't happen.

In December, 2001 I had a group of Evan's friends over to our house and I asked them what they thought success was. Having money seemed to be a popular response. I then asked them if they thought Mother Theresa was successful. They knew that, yes, she was successful, but now they were confused. I could see the wheels turning in their teenage minds. Confusion and curiosity are the first steps toward finding the answers to our questions. Life is a journey and we all must start with the first step. The next step, if you are the kind that wants some answers, is to start thinking and searching.

Many people, especially young people, are searching for something that they don't understand and cannot fathom .What is it they are looking for and where can it be found? And we wonder why so many teenagers are unhappy? The same could easily be said for many adults as well. I wish the young people could take a close look at the people around them and imagine their future if they followed the same path. Who is the happiest of them all? Most of us don't share our innermost feelings and project the image we want others to see, not necessarily the truth, therefore we can't tell if someone is happy from external appearances.

We also can't judge those who would be able to provide us with wisdom, as there isn't a halo over their heads, and there isn't a "look" that enlightened people have, contrary to popular opinion.

Another gauge of how we are doing is the mirror test. I think that we see ourselves in other people; and we can tell the type of person we are by looking at how we view most other people. I have found that crooks tend to think everyone else is a crook, nice people tend to think other people are nice, mean people think others are mean, and so on. I have found this test to be quite reliable.

Preparing to die

April 4

Death is certain, but why do we avoid this subject like the plague? Do we think that by not talking about death it will somehow bypass us? Do we talk about our impending death at parties and ask, "*So, how are you preparing for your death and the death of your loved ones?*"

If we can't start thinking and preparing for our death, then we cannot complete our life, because death is part of our life, it's just the end—of our physical life. It's not an accident that we are the only species that is aware that we will die. Don't you wonder sometimes why we have such knowledge? What would life be like if we didn't realize that we were going to die one day? Animals see other animals die and don't associate it with their own demise; nor do we, it seems, until it is too late.

We grieve when someone dies before they reach old age. Rightfully so. People still get upset when someone older dies, but it is the fate of us all. However, I can certainly understand missing someone when they are gone. Lately, I get more upset about people that fail to *live* than when someone dies. Dying is easy— it's living that is hard. To die, ultimately, all we have to do is to let go; but to live we have so many things to discover and experience, so many adventures to go on, and so many lessons to learn. Many of those discoveries and adventures will be difficult to accomplish, but nonetheless, they are worthy of our best efforts.

Parents typically don't talk to their children about death, since we want to protect them from thoughts and images that would be morbid and depressing. We want our kids to be happy, so why talk to them about death? After all, we don't want to scare them, or make them unhappy. By not talking with our spouses, our children, our friends and loved ones about this most important subject, we rob them of the opportunity to face up to the fact that we are mortal, and one day, will in fact, die. Focusing on the end of our life can help us understand that we need to be prepared for our demise. By preparing to die, just as it is for any other important thing we must do, it will assist us in doing a better job; in this case a better job of *living* our life.

Preparation helps us achieve better grades on schoolwork, we know from experience. We also know that when a project comes up at work, and we are prepared, we will accomplish more and do a better job. When we have a game to play we know that by preparing we will hopefully play a better game, and maybe even win the game. When it comes to death however, we don't prepare.. Seemingly, death will last a while, so you would think that death would require the most preparation.

Someone recently asked me *"How do you prepare for death? Is it something about making out your will and stuff like that*?" It's a good question, and I would assume most people wouldn't know exactly what it means to be prepared to die. To me, it means living your life as if you only had one week left to live, and living that way for the rest of your life. Taking care of all your unfinished business is of prime importance, such as saying what you need to say to the people you care about. Forgiving people, making up, resolving conflicts, saying you're sorry, telling people how much you love or care for them. Doing what you should be doing. Finding what you were searching for. These are all part of the unfinished business that should never be unfinished, no matter how old we are, because we don't know when our time on this earth will be ended.

Talk to your loved ones straight from your heart, hold nothing back, tell them what you would tell them if you weren't going to be around shortly—except you're not dying—or are you? We are dying, little by little every day. Also, since most of us don't know when we are going to die, it seems prudent to be prepared. This isn't a morbid subject, because if you prepare to die, you will *live* your life. It's a positive message, not a negative one.

Preparing to die is not putting things off until the timing is better. The right moment may never come, or you may simply run out of time.

There is a certain feeling associated with taking care of unfinished business. It's a state of mental well being: nothing has been left unfinished or unsaid—nothing is nagging for completion. How can we know what our unfinished business is? Typically, those people and situations in our life that are causing us the most pain and suffering are the unfinished business. Unfortunately, it is just those people and those scenarios that are the most painful that we need to resolve. We have to be honest enough with ourselves to uncover the pain to see where we need to go, with regard to who, and what is causing us the pain. Then take care of it!

Door Opening

April 9

When Evan died, it was as if one door closed and another opened. It was quite a shock to see the door open and walk through it metaphorically speaking. I guess it was some kind of cosmic compensation for the loss of our son. It takes surrender and acceptance of the closed door in order for us to be able to see the open door and walk through it.

In my case, another door did open and it provided a different perspective on this life and why we are here on earth. I am not positive that this is "*the* answer, because there is no way to validate it, but it does feel right. A level of understanding that I never had before has been provided to me, and all of the pieces seem to fit together as if a puzzle that I didn't know existed was being constructed and suddenly appeared before me with a vision of how the parts connect. Our job is to realize there is a puzzle, which is called our life, and to solve it or to figure out how the pieces connect. At minimum, there is something each one of us needs to do in this life, which is the primary reason we are on this earth—to learn certain lessons and connect with our true self.

I saw that everything is as it should be; we need only to understand that. If we could accept what is given to us, we can learn from both the "good" and the "bad." Our "gifts" and "tragedies" are actually equal in value, in that we can learn the lessons we need to learn from either the "good" or the "bad." Actually if you look closer there is really no "good" or "bad" if we can learn the lessons we need to learn from both, then the reality is that it's only our perception that something is good or bad. Is a bad experience bad if we are able to gain understanding and knowledge from it? Of course, there may be pain associated with a "bad" experience, but isn't that how we grow—by breaking through the pain to a new level of awareness?

It takes a bit of getting used to, but if we could look at things objectively, we could understand that we are getting gifts all the time, in the sense that these gifts are the messengers which provide us with situations we can learn from. They come in different packages with various wrappings, but if we can learn or gain understanding of this life and how we need to live it from all experiences, then everything is a gift.

Of course, there is sadness associated with some "gifts," as none of us are that evolved that we can separate our emotions from the lessons we are receiving. That is particularly true in my case.

It appears that we are here on this earth to learn lessons that we need to learn and that is why we have been placed in the family we have, surrounded by the situations that confront us, and born into the status we desired in order to have the maximum learning experience. We can only learn our lessons however, if we are aware that we are supposed to learn from our situations.

Whether we were born into riches or poverty, have loving parents or awful ones, experience more heartache than joy, it doesn't matter, since we can learn what we need to learn from what we are given. The grass is only greener on the other side because of the lessons that need to be learned from those people with the greener grass. The grass isn't greener, it's always just right and appropriate for each individual on earth.

> *"You and God picked your own parents out of a choice of a billion! You chose them so you can help them to grow and learn and they can be your teachers too. Life is like a school where we are given a chance to learn many things-like to get along with other people, or to understand our feelings, to learn to be honest with ourselves and others, to learn to give and receive love-and when we have passed all the tests-(just like in school)-we are allowed to graduate-that means we are allowed to return to our real home-To God"*
> *— Elisabeth Kübler-Ross, M.D. from a Letter to Dougy*

I realize this may not be your understanding; it's mine and I gained my understanding through a process that is beyond me to comprehend. It really isn't intellectual in nature at all. It isn't as if I figured things out by studying the various religious texts and researching all known information about our life on earth. There were some books however, that were quite helpful in my need to understand the bigger picture. Understanding of universal truths is not only designed for people with high IQs. The "truth" is for everyone, regardless of their circumstances or intellectual capacity.

Also, my understanding is via my life experiences as well, and those are relevant only to me, not to anyone else. Everything that has ever happened to me has helped me in some way to formulate my current understanding. We can learn from others, but realistically, our understanding has to come from within us. We cannot take another person's understanding and make it our own, no matter how hard we may try.

Knowledge

April 15

This whole life is a gift that many of us have never unwrapped. We act like the gift is the wrapping, so we never bother to look inside the packaging. That is a fairly accurate statement, as most people do not understand that the true gift is actually inside of us. How to go inside and find the gift is another matter entirely. Just saying it's inside is both true and somewhat of a tease. I mean the gift is literally inside us, not figuratively. Many spiritual and religious people, as well as the scriptures, say that there is a treasure inside of us, but without actually being able to access the treasure, we have only our ideas and thoughts about what the treasure might be. What good is a treasure if you can't get to it? A treasure made up of ideas and concepts isn't real. I can't spend conceptual money at the store, so why is a conceptual version of the truth any more real?

The treasure inside would appear to be what many of us have been searching for, not knowing that it has been inside of us all along. Everywhere we have gone looking for this "something,"—we carried it within us. This treasure is *the* antidote for unhappiness. What is inside of us that is so great? It's the true experience of love, which is different from the kind of love that is associated with people or things. It's love, as you have never experienced it before. Pure love, unadulterated by this world.

Many years ago I was searching for peace and happiness. I wasn't sure which one I was actually looking for, peace or happiness—or were they the same? I read just about everything that I could stand reading on those subjects and decided, as I indicated earlier, that words alone were not sufficient for me to become satisfied.

I tried drugs, but they weren't the answer I was looking for, although it took a while for me to figure that out. Once, I spent almost a year in a mountain chalet in Colorado, just thinking about life, and reading spiritual books. After some time, I realized that *"I* wanted the same experiences that the writers of those books were talking about. Why couldn't I have been born thousands of years ago, when all the action seemed to be taking place?" I thought." Why did I have to be content to read about someone else's great experiences?" I wanted those experiences myself—now—in my lifetime.

How was I going to get those experiences? I really had no clue. I knew that I really wanted to find this thing called inner peace. But how do you go inside and find it? What's "inside?" How can peace be found within? Is it just a concept, or a philosophy? All I knew at that time, was that I didn't have peace. Knowing that it was within me did nothing to help me. In fact it made me more frustrated, because, if it was within me, how could I enjoy it? I was as frustrated and unhappy as I have ever been in my life.

Many people say they have the answer, and if you just believe in their philosophy or religion then you would have *"the* ultimate truth. Believe, accept, have faith. Since I could only believe, not experience what they were talking about, there was no way for me to test which was the correct path. How can you test or validate a belief? You can't.

After all, picking the right path is important but how are you going to pick the right one when the signs for all paths say, "this is the right way?" People that simply accept that their chosen path or religion is the ultimate answer, never having looked at other paths for comparison, may be missing something. That would be like marrying the first person you ever dated, which as we all know isn't the smartest thing to do, since we understand that it is by comparison and contrasting that we can formulate a reliable method to figure out if something is right for us.

After getting really fed up with not being able to find anyone or any book that could actually give me something other than words telling me to "have faith," I heard the words of a young man named Prem Rawat in 1973. He is also known as Maharaji, which is an honorary title. Since the age of eight years old he has been speaking around the world on the subject of inner knowledge, speaking to millions of people in his lifetime. Maharaji said that he could *show* me this inner experience. I could learn how to actually go inside and experience my essence. But this wasn't something to believe in; either you had the experience or you didn't. Now that sounded really good to me because I didn't have to believe in something or "have faith." No books I had ever read, or any person I had spoken to or heard of mentioned that an experience was available for me, not just for people that were lucky enough to live in the time of Jesus, Buddha, Krishna, or Mohammed, et all.

> *"The peace you are looking for is within you and I can help you find it. I 'm not preaching to people, and I am not here to tell them what is good or bad, right or wrong, or what to do. What I offer is not a religion, and it is compatible with all religions. I am not doing this for financial gain, and what I offer is not for sale. This a gift, in the truest tradition of a gift."*
> *— Compilation of Prem Rawat (Maharaji) message*

> *"If you would like to find that contentment within you, I offer a way to do so. I am not proposing solutions to world problems. I have no certificates to back up what I am saying. I have only one thing riding on my side, and that is the heart. Listen to me only if your heart concurs. Otherwise, don't."*
> *— Maharaji.*

Well, I followed up this method of "going inside" which Maharaji calls Self Knowledge. I can't reveal exactly what happened, as the information is not for publication, because there is a certain level of understanding necessary in order to receive the ability to go within. It would be similar to giving someone diamonds, but because they didn't understand the value of the diamonds, they threw them away or traded them for a little food. I can however say that nothing was given to me as this essence already existed inside of me. No one can give you what lies within you; they can only help you find it. How many people do you know that can help you literally see who and what you really are?

> *"There is this light, which you can turn off leaving the darkness. Then there is the universe, and in the universe, there is the light of stars and the sun. And the absence of those also leads to darkness. This light can illuminate this hall, but it cannot illuminate the earth. The sun, on the other hand, has the power to illuminate the earth, while a candle only has the power to*

> *illuminate a little area.*
>
> *And then, there is another kind of light, and that is your light, the light within you, the light of Knowledge, the light of understanding. And the darkness that the light within gets rid of can never be got rid of by these external lights. Even the sun cannot get rid of the darkness of ignorance. Nuclear bombs going off — they create light, too. But nothing can get rid of the darkness of ignorance, except for one thing — the light within."*
> *— Edited excerpt, Maharaji 2nd May 2001*

The Creator, in its wisdom planted the remedy for what ails us inside of us, and the funny thing is that some of us look everywhere for something that has already been given to us. We need only to learn how to focus our attention inside and then we will find what we need and want, instead of focusing on what we were looking for in external things.

When I was shown how to go within I did experience seeing who I was. I mean literally, seeing. There is an Inner Light that is visible with your eyes closed. It's not an illusion. When people long ago referred to "seeing the light," they weren't referring to a new understanding. They were seeing the light! There are also other internal experiences that we can focus our attention on. Once I had this inner experience I knew I had found what I had been looking for all these years; not a philosophy or a belief, but a true inner experience, as opposed to a thought or belief. I could actually have an experience, verifiable through my senses. I knew this inner experience was "true" immediately upon feeling it. My searching ended, almost 30 years ago. I became a *finder* instead of a seeker.

I think many of us theorize that this thing we call peace, or inner peace is a figment of speech, or a peace that is obtained by reading books; an intellectual understanding of inner peace, which has nothing to do with an actual inner experience. Since most of us think a real inner experience in our lifetime is impossible, we don't look for it, and that's precisely why we don't find it. This experience has nothing to do with religion, or philosophy which if you thought about it, is the way it should be.

The way to experience this inner dimension is to meditate. Meditate simply means to focus on something. Why not focus on what the Creator intended you to focus on, after all it was put inside of you to find and enjoy. As St. Francis of Assisi said *"prayer is when we talk to God and meditation is when we listen."*

Of course there are those who insist they know all about going within as they too have experienced this inner realm through their study of their religious texts. There is no use debating with people that aren't open.

The next morning, after being given the ability to go within, I awoke filled with so much love I could barely function. I was experiencing something that I had never, ever felt before. The love inside that I was feeling was so overpowering that I could only enjoy it. I thought this has to be the feeling that is described as Nirvana in some scriptures. I had never felt this good in my life. I was feeling love for everything, not associated or related to a person, which was quite a new experience for me. This feeling isn't part of my everyday experience unfortunately, but I was shown that the love inside is so vast and so powerful, that it is certainly worthwhile to try again and again to go within, which I do.

During the first week of my meditation on my inner self, I had a realization that we are like gold miners looking for gold in a tunnel. We have our pick-axes and we *know* that there is a gold vein and we are digging and digging. I thought that if I gave up, I could only be one pick-axe stroke away from discovering the gold, so why stop? This is like our quest for what we are looking for. Why stop? We could have been looking for years and then stop, being one minute, one day, one breath away from finding what we were searching for. We must go on until we find what we need to find, unless of course, we are spectators instead of players, seekers instead of finders.

Having this experience isn't the end, it's the beginning. Realizing that exercise makes us feel better is good, but actually exercising is better, and exercising just once will not either get or keep us in shape. Meditation is the same, in that it's something that we can do everyday, and the more we meditate and partake in that beauty inside, the more we benefit. The experience of meditation on this inner experience is very peaceful in the truest sense of the word, as more and more of our thoughts about life, work, kids, and stuff that drives us crazy will slowly disappear. There is only silence, and that silence is the most beautiful feeling I have ever experienced in my whole life.

For me the key to unlocking this "inner peace" mystery was Maharaji. On my own, I am confident that I would never have found it. This may be difficult to comprehend, but for me that's that way it was.

You can find more information on Prem Rawat on his website:www.tprf.org.

> *"We can forgive a child who is afraid of the dark; the real tragedy of life is when men are afraid of the light."*
> *— Plato*

> *"The religion of the future will be a cosmic religion. The religion which is based on experience."*
> *— Albert Einstein*

Drugs:

April 26

I don't condone the use of drugs, but having taken them for a number of years, (mostly marijuana), I find that the current state of anti-drug campaigns are woefully inadequate with regard to reaching teens who are tempted to try them. Teenagers take drugs because they want an experience that is more exciting than their current experience of life. They want something that alters their state of being, similar to the appeal of alcohol for adults. Many of the people who are involved in the anti-drug movement have little or no experience with drugs, and they don't understand their appeal or the effects they have on the user.

When the drug message is that drugs are bad, while those people that are using soft drugs such as marijuana tell their friends that drugs are actually good, there is a real credibility problem. Who do you think the kids will believe, their friends who have tried the drugs or the adults who haven't?

Speaking from my experience, I have found that meditation on your inner self is a great alternative to drugs. The meditation I refer to is not to be confused with TM, or any number of other forms of meditation requiring the meditator to chant words or similar practices. The experience of meditation is much higher than drugs, and won't create the problems that are inherent in drug use. Drug educators need to face the facts that drugs are enjoyable, thus their appeal. We need to find something to offer to kids that is more enjoyable than drugs to stop the rampant drug use. There is no other way, regardless of how anti-drug educators may feel. Of course, drug education is helpful, and I understand the need for the message that drugs are dangerous, which they can be. I lost my best friend to drugs, so I have certainly seen the dark side of this issue.

When I first started taking drugs in the mid 1960s, it was to increase my spiritual awareness. That's the truth. After a period of time, I realized that my drug use wasn't getting me to the place that I had originally envisioned, and I quit. I am very glad that I quit when I did, and would not encourage kids to try drugs, but we need to be realistic.

To focus on the experience that deep meditation brings will decrease drug use and increase respect for others because when we have this deep inner experience we can recognize that we are all the same, thus it would be in our best interest to treat others with respect and kindness. Again, this is from my experience. It isn't just a theory.

I had always thought about what I would say to Evan when he asked about drugs, which would have been inevitable. I would tell him that I tried drugs, which he already had figured out, since I had attended Woodstock and he had seen the movie where it showed rampant drug use. Evan also knew that since I was a hippie I had most likely taken a ride on the wild side, which would have been absolutely correct.

If I would have lied to Evan about drugs, all of the credibility that I had built up over the years would have been lost. I would have told him that I was really searching for an experience that made me higher than my normal consciousness and that I thought taking drugs was the answer. I found out that drugs weren't the answer, and if you weren't careful they could either ruin or end your life. He would have been skeptical, but I would have focused on the experience he was seeking. I don't think kids are actually attracted to drugs, but to the experience that they provide if you can understand the distinction. Drugs are simply a perceived way to get a "high." It's the experience that is being sought not the delivery system. There are many people that find athletics, music, art, or other pursuits provide a "high," and rightfully so. But what happens if you aren't artistic or athletic? Kids want to be high. So do adults. There isn't anything wrong with that. They just need to find the right way to get to the place they want to be without drugs.

If people want to be high in order to feel better they need to find the high that was already built into them. The Creator already figured this one out. People naturally want a higher state of consciousness, so the remedy was placed inside of us. It's free, easily accessible, isn't illegal, doesn't require a college education, and is available to all that seek the highest high there is.

Openness

May 1

We have a feeling that something is missing in our life but we don't know what we are searching for. This is the problem. How can we find something if we don't know what it is? We just have to hope and pray that we are open, since being closed will only limit our sight We definitely need the sight to see what cannot be seen, and feel what cannot be understood, and hear what is not meant to be heard by external ears.

An open mind is very helpful in this process. If we close our minds and hearts to things we do not intellectually understand, we might never find what we are searching for. We will only find what we *want* to find, not what we were *meant* to find: there is a huge difference between what we want and what we are destined for.

If we don't know where to find the information that can help us in our journey, it pays to be open to everything. We can always use our own brain and powers of observation and filtering to determine if something is worthy of further study. Therefore, we need not fear investigation, just as we cannot judge a book by its cover, we cannot completely evaluate or assess anything unless we investigate it, especially when it concerns our spiritual life, and our potential happiness.

With traditional religion you simply have to have faith, because there is no real credible evidence, so we have to believe. What would a legal trial be like if the same criteria were used? Since there is no real evidence, I'd have to believe either the defense attorney or prosecution attorney since they would not have anything more than ideas and possible motives—no facts that can be tested. I don't think any of us would agree to a system of justice like that, so why should we agree to a spiritual reality that is similar?

> *"In old days, people would build castles, which in a war would be besieged. But if the castle was well- provisioned, it would withstand it. Sometimes a king would even divert little streams*

from underground to where they were so they would have a fresh supply of water inside the castle.

Have you stocked well in your castle? When the enemy lays siege, how long are you going to last? Stock well with your inner wealth. Be familiar with this breath. Know how to tap its tranquility. Don't forget that. This breath is full of joy-not the kind of joy our mind wants, but rich in the joy that your heart wants.. And if you know how to, you can outlast any siege. Within you is a thirst-quenching water-not H20, but a different kind of water which quenches a very different kind of thirst.

Because time has laid its siege on you. War is afoot. Death is camped outside. Should you be scared? Of course not, because hopefully, you've stocked well. Time has come to steal you And it lays siege, but relax. It's okay if you know how to go within. Everything you need is there. Good news? Very. You don't have to be paranoid, don't have to be afraid. Stock well. In every breath find everything you've always looked for. Laugh, because you can afford to laugh. Laugh from the very depths of your being, because you have experienced joy. Become unwavering to that heart. Become devoted to that clarity. Become a student of understanding."

— Maharaji, San Diego, California Nov., 2001

Being Awake

The real fight is between being asleep and being awake. Many of us spend our lives living in a dream state, somewhere between sleep, being awake and dreaming. It was our heritage as children to be awake and look at the world through innocent eyes, where there are no limits and nothing is impossible. We knew then what was important. We were in touch with something wonderful; we were experiencing it, not thinking about it.

Gradually, as we get older, our childlike innocence was slowly covered up by the residue of life, which clouds our vision. It makes us sleepier and sleepier until we think that finding what we wanted to find isn't even on our agenda, and the forgetfulness begins. When we have forgotten and misplaced our vision, we are lost, as if a great fog has descended into our world and we can't see what is beyond the pale curtain in front of us. We eventually decide that there isn't anything worthwhile beyond the fog and we may as well get used to the world encased by fog. After all, we should make the best of any situation, right? Right, but there are situations where making the best of something isn't acceptable. We need to understand the situations in which we are destined to go beyond what seems like a stone wall, are but in reality, only fog.

When I speak of being awake, I am speaking about understanding how to live our lives productively, in tune with what we need to learn, and finding the way to connect to our inner self.

How can you know that you are awake? You will know, however you won't know when you are asleep; that's the scary part. Is there a test to find out our waking status? There isn't. When, and if you somehow you find the way to awaken, you will realize the dream state you were living in wasn't a nightmare and wasn't bliss. It was just moving through your life not realizing or understanding the purpose of situations or appreciating the life we have been given— which is our gift, to help us learn our lessons— if we have the right perspective.

Friends: Questions and Answers?

May 4

Evan's friends were an integral and beneficial part of his life. They were from a mixture of groups and cliques, and quite diverse. There were many in his outer circle, but only a few in his inner circle. I think had he lived longer, the number of people in the inner circle would have grown significantly, because he was just beginning to appreciate the value of good conversation and was interested in surrounding himself with people whom he liked, irrespective of their status or coolness.

His friends are now struggling with their own mortality, brought into closer view by Evan's death. So many questions, and no one to talk to who can help them sort out what is unrealistic and what is realistic, except the few lucky enough to be seen by therapists, which can be of great help (if you have a great therapist). I feel sorry for any young person looking for answers about the big questions in life who has no one to talk to. It is a lonely feeling, one that I am quite familiar with. Young adults have a tough time as it is, especially if they are adventurers, who will not settle for the watered down version of life many adults offer.

The voices of his friends after the tragedy, and almost certainly before were full of agony— the agony of youth searching for meaning, yet finding none.

> *"I lead a life of pain and sorrow*
> *I'll live tonight but I dread tomorrow*
> *The pain can kill me, it already did*
> *I guess my life is over and I'm only a kid*
> *Depression has taken me*
> *Where no one else will go*
> *Now soon I'll end my own life*
> *But no one will ever know*
> *That I'm sorry for what I have done*
> *Though I don't regret my choices*
> *I'm at the mercy of myself*

Commanded by the voices
The voices in my head
That pulls me inside out
The voices inside
They turned whispers into shouts
Shouts that I am useless
A pointless waste of space
The medicine is suicide
For my special case
So I'll leave with I love u
Always and forever
I hope someday I'll meet you
At the end of my endeavor"

— (The person who wrote this poem is fine. Don't worry)

Such pain, from such a beautiful young person. They don't yet understand how beautiful they are, and where the true beauty can be found. But they will, or at least they can if pointed in the right direction. The rest is up to them.

In December of 2001, I got together with some of Evan's friends and asked them to talk about what was bothering them. They wanted to know what happens when you die, and if there is a heaven. I started thinking about their question. When we were younger there were a few childhood myths that our parents fostered, like the tooth fairy. First there was a tooth fairy, and then there wasn't. Then there was Santa Claus, then there wasn't. Perhaps there was also the Easter Bunny and the Sandman. Now, when our parents tell us not to worry about dying, because if we lead a "good" life, we will go to heaven. Hmmm. Teenagers are looking very closely at that response and wondering if it will turn out like the tooth fairy or Santa Claus. It would be natural to assume that connecting the dots should lead you to that place. What is one to believe when we have been lied to about important myths in our life and then told "well, we were just trying to protect you to keep the magic alive." As a parent, I did the same thing.

Evan's friends do not yet truly understand the cycle of birth and death and our purpose on earth. So it has been hard for them to assess whether his life had simply been cut short unnecessarily, or was his death part of a bigger plan, one which we cannot fully understand, only accept? Some of the parents told their children to "just get over it," which is horrible advice. They will never get over it, but they can go on with their lives. The parents' advice just made the kids feel even more alienated from them.

It saddened me to know that many of the kids were depressed, although I can understand why. I felt badly that their parents either couldn't or didn't talk to them about their depression and in some cases were simply unaware that the depression existed. It is difficult for parents to communicate with teenagers, because teenagers usually don't want to have anything to do with their parents. Their friends can't help either, as they are typically at the same level of understanding.

To be at the beginning of your life (teenagers), and to not understand the mission and journey that we each need to undertake, and to not have the right perspective, is a sad state of affairs. There is so much to learn, but we can't learn if we don't have anyone to point the way to the starting gate. This is basically the point where the big questions begin. Parents can't help not knowing what they don't know, however they do bear some of the blame if they have never looked for the truth, and just settled on some belief that was handed down from their parents and never questioned.

> *"What's the point? You search for happiness, yet spend your entire life looking; achieving nothing because there's no such thing as true happiness. Why do people who want to die live on and the people who love life die?"*
> *— a friend*

The teenagers I know who are questioning the status quo tend to be the more sensitive, artistic types, who look at life differently from their peers. It is sad enough for them to have to go through so much pain and suffering thinking there are no answers, when there are. How depressing it must be to be suffering and think that there is no relief, when there is.

> *"Along with Evan's death I have also had a member of my family die. You would think I would be used to mortality, I don't think I ever will be. Nor will anyone, but it's a fact of life we all have to deal with. With all these deaths and all the sorrow in my life, I have found myself in a depression that I can't seem to escape from. I can't exactly pinpoint what started it, but I believe it was life itself."*
> *— a friend*

I believe that eventually most kids will get to the bigger questions about life and death and the purpose of life, but once they run into a wall they will quickly retreat to a safe belief system and stop questioning. They are likely to become as their parents, and that might be okay. For others it won't be. They'll be the ones who challenge the status quo.

> *"I know that this unimaginable pain cannot be relived in any way for you, but I hope that it helps you to know that the people in your community, and not even just Evan's closest friends, are sharing the terrible pain as well as the incredibly joyful images of the happiest, proudest, most content child I have ever known."*
> *— mother of a friend*

The following is a book report based on the rough draft of this book. The person who wrote this report is in 9th grade and didn't know Evan. His mother is a friend of mine:

Question #1
Why is the character you read about admirable?

> Evan Holofcener was the main character of the book, and I don't know how a 13 kid could be more admired. Evan was so admirable he had such passion, desire, all these wonderful qualities that I wish I had, Evan was only 13. Evan loved music and was a very gifted musician with a guitar, he would sit every night, go on the internet and force himself to learn new songs, I

admire that patience and knack for music. Over the summer Evan only ate healthy foods and drunk mainly water so he could clear up his bad case of acne. His persistence and ability to not waver from his goal is what I admire. Evan was a vegetarian, his respect and appreciation for animals is something that I agree with, but I have grown up as meat being my main diet and don't see how I could stop eating it now, but Evan had the ability and power. Evan was a wonderful poet, he could write his thoughts onto paper and make them flow and connect beautifully, I admire his poetic ability and not being afraid to share his feelings like that. Evan was a great, nice, caring friend to all. I know I will admire him.

Question #2
What one quality was extraordinary about the main character in your book?

Evan had desire, he had a whole lot of it. Evan's desire drove him to do the things he wanted to do, not put them off or ignore them. He knew he could accomplish anything he wanted and that gave him power. Evan's desire must have filled all the holes in his life as he could do anything he set his mind to. Everyone's life could be complete if we all were just more like Evan. I wish I had the desire to do the things I truly wanted to do, but I know I feel like it because I have Evan. I just keep gaining a little more even if the people around me don't notice.

Question #3
You read about someone who actually lived. in what ways did this person demonstrate universal, human qualities?

Evan was a role model for all. Evan is physically described in the book, he sounds like an example of what boys want to be like. Naturally smart, very strong, athletic, and good looking. Evan was a caring, nice, smart kid, something many people strive to be or I wished they did. A world of Evan's would be a great place. Each person has different qualities and Evan had his own superb ones, I don't think you can characterize them as human qualities since many humans don't have those things. Evan was a super kid.

Question # 4
Did the character you read about make a difference in the lives of others- or in his surroundings or world- in any way? if so explain-

Evan impacted everyone around him, and he will continue to do so through this book. Evan had an unusual passion and desire for everything he did, when people saw this it was almost slightly passed on. Now that he is not with us it feels like when you do something with passion you're doing it for Evan, he is that motivation that can push to you to great things. Evan put the passion and love back into many peoples lives. When Evan died, all of Groton was shocked and saddened. His death depressed and affected the small town, whether the people knew him or not they knew he was a great kid and the world would never be the same. Evan put the beauty into the world, I know Evan impacted me through the way he lived his life. I strive to learn from him. Evan I wish I knew you, I never knew you but you still seem to almost be a part of me. Why? Gods speed my friend.

I really liked reading the book and I hope I get to read future copies, maybe next time I will be smart enough to have a pencil on hand to take notes with on the book. Thank you I will never forget Evan and I'm glad I got to know him even though he doesn't know me.

Letters

In the *Groton Herald* Newspaper, in January of 2002 they printed a list of the top stories of 2001. The following is a letter to the editor dated January 11, 2002.

Dear Editor:

"The Groton Herald conspicuously left out the tragic death of Evan Holofcener in its mention of the most significant events in the past year. There is hardly a day that goes by when I do not look at my own children and thank God that they are healthy and well, and the untimely death of Evan has certainly been a more significant factor in my life than the increasing value of my home."

Letters from mothers

There were a number of mothers who wrote to us about how Evan's death affected them and their families. Here are two examples.

Letters from Moms:

(1)

"Mark is starting to write about Evan, the impact of his short life had on kids he knew both well and hardly at all. More impact than people had who were several times his age. I'm still listening, learning a lot about grace under extreme pressure, taking comfort (who needs comfort here?) from a father's assurance that there is meaning here that can't be lost. In fact it has to be explored, dissected, passed on to those of us who just motion through our lives believing everything will be okay. In fact it's possible that nothing will ever be okay, that some higher level of pain and introspection is what we need to kick-start the real purpose of our lives.

For me, the fall of 2001 was Before and After. For most people it will be before and after Sept. 11th. But Evan's death was the dividing line for me. It scared me to the corner of my being. Forced me to take on pain suddenly real. Reminded me of how lucky I am and how quickly that can change. How important it is to connect with people, to give something of yourself that is given—even if and when you go away."

(2)

"At the time of Evan's death I felt that my life was pretty well set. My kids were all playing with their friends enjoying the beautiful summer day. My husband and I were working in our yard as usual. Then our lives suddenly changed. My phone rang and a neighbor told me the horrible news. I was shaken beyond words trying to comprehend what I had heard. How could this happen on such a beautiful day? How could this happen to an innocent child? How could this happen to someone in our own neighborhood? Evan was the same age as my oldest son. This could have just as easily my own family's tragedy. Why Evan? Why this family?

It is a parent's worst fear. Even as I write this nearly three months later, my heart still aches and my tears continue to flow. I still have so many questions, but I'm beginning to accept that I may never know the answers, at least while my spirit lives in this body, here on earth.

So when the same neighbor called just a few hours later asking if I could come to their house and drive with them to be at the hospital (morgue) with Evan again, I didn't hesitate to go. It was the absolute least I could do for them. It was also the hardest, most difficult thing that I was ever to do in my life and I pray that I am never called upon to help someone in that way ever again. This was to be the beginning of my "awakened" life.

Before, I had been going along living my life in my beautiful new home, doing the things I thought I should do and saying the things I thought I should say, but really just doing and not really thinking. Now, all that I said and did really seemed to matter. And as I spent more time with Nancy and Mark I was so impressed and awed with their love, their strength and their courage.

I drew strength from them and was able to return that strength empowered to help them. Over the next few days I experienced many things that I never imagined I would experience. Where do you begin to plan a memorial service for your beloved thirteen-year old son? The legal and business decisions that needed to be made seemed ludicrous. This can't be happening! During this time I also experienced some of the most wonderful and precious experiences of my life. I saw many people in our neighborhood and town come together for a family that they hardly knew.

In this tragedy, I was finding love and compassion that I had rarely felt before. Every emotion was on a new level. We parents would sit around in disbelief, reflecting on our relationships with our own children. Evan had such a close relationship with both his parents; could we say the same? I, thankfully, feel that I do have such a relationship. Would my children answer the same? I can tell you that we have talked about this in our house and it has been gratifying. Nancy and Mark have been so committed to their family, consciously aware of the impact of their parenting on their children. Because of their awareness, they can fortunately reflect and feel good about their decisions they made together and the experiences they have allowed their children to explore.

Evan's memorial service was held at the Unitarian Universalist church in our town. It was the first time I had attended this parish, as it was for many others sitting in the pews around me. I was so moved by words spoken from the heart. So many children there to say good bye to a friend. So many words that they wished they had spoken to Evan just a week before. I was struck at how

Evan had touched so many lives in thirteen brief years.

Mark's eulogy was incredible, once again exemplifying the love and strength that I had been privileged to experience in the previous days.

It has been only recently that I have come to realize how interdependent life and death truly are. That may sound silly, but I truly felt that the two were separate entities. I knew, of course, that if you lived a "good" life you would go to Heaven, but that was that. The complexity our spiritual growth that spans beyond measure of time as we know it was still unknown to me. I now believe that there is definitely much more for us than our lives here on Earth, but what we do with our lives is of utmost importance. Through talking and learning and reading and experiencing spirituality, I am much more comforted, and excited even, at the prospect of a long spiritual life. We are truly never alone and our spirits never die. I believe now that we each have important jobs to fulfill in our lives and yet we have much more to learn and experience once our spirit leaves our body.

I don't feel that I make a conscious decision to be with Nancy and Mark each day, it's just where I am meant to be at this time. The support and friendship I give to them is nothing compared to the nurturing, support, and friendship that they give to me. I am amazed every day where my life is directed and redirected. My soul and my spirit are growing and are uplifted.

Thank you Evan for entering my life."

My background

I thought it would be useful to know a little about me, as my background and perspective is certainly evident in this book

I was happy for the most part growing up, in spite of the fact that that my parents were mean to me. I didn't get it. I didn't do anything to deserve this, I thought. Both my father and mother were quite bad when it came to parenting (they would have agreed). Being in this family taught me a multitude of lessons. The lessons I learned were hard on me, but nonetheless, I learned very early on what I didn't want to become, and how I didn't want to treat other people when I was older. It's better to have positive role models, but I didn't have that option. I was more determined than you can imagine to growing up differently from the behavior of my parents. I worked very hard to become a different kind of person than my father which I have accomplished, although I am much, much more than simply the opposite of my father. My father tried as hard as he could to take away my sense of pride and accomplishment. He never succeeded, but it wasn't for lack of trying. Since I learned first-hand how it felt to be mistreated, I wanted to treat my own kids differently and never inflict the same hurt I felt on them. I have been true to my word, as my kids would attest to.

Growing up in a family that believed that money was the path to happiness, it was refreshingly clear to me by the age of 12, that money wasn't making my parents or their friends happy. My parents weren't rich but lived quite well, as did their friends. I was confused. If money is supposed to be so great, why wasn't it making the people I knew happy? I thought the point of making money was to make you happy! Finally, I did understand via a revelation, my first one, that money wasn't the key to happiness. Wow!! Now what was I supposed to do with my life? I thought there was a formula that you followed that would provide you what you wanted out of life: go to college, get a good job, make money, be happy, and then retire. At least that is what I had been told. My whole world was turned upside down. If money wasn't making people happy, what was? I was really upset and confused about my life plans and I didn't have anyone to talk to at that time or throughout my childhood.

Ultimately, I would have to figure things out myself, which I did. It was a difficult position to be in, because I now knew what I didn't want, but not what I did want! I wouldn't recommend that mindset, as it was both a painful and confusing state to be in, but I didn't have any choice. Once I started thinking about this money thing, I started questioning everything. I learned that other things that I was taking for granted weren't all that I thought they should or would be. Now what?

My questioning of life and ideas began in earnest. I felt differently from those who were going along with "the program." In the 1950s, most everyone went along with what their parents wanted, and wanted for them. I was different, and remain so today.

I went to the University of Maryland, but became so bored that I dropped out short of graduating. I still didn't know what I wanted to do with myself and with my life. I eventually got a job selling carpeting wholesale. I managed to become the best salesman in the company, and soon I was making more money than I knew what to do with. It was good to know that if I applied myself I could do well at something, and selling seemed to come naturally to me. I wasn't sure if I was good at anything prior to this experience. I was soon offered the hottest job in the carpet business, and became the industry's youngest mill rep. I flourished in this environment and through a combination of hard work and natural ability I became a big success, something that I thought I didn't want to be, since I was equating making money with being successful. There was also the good feeling I had about accomplishing my goals, and exceeding them. It was cool though. I have to be honest about it. There isn't anything wrong with making money. It's just the perception that money will solve all of the problems of life that is the problem.

The next thing I knew, I was living in a penthouse apartment just below Georgetown in Washington, D.C. I drove a customized Pontiac convertible (considered cool at the time) and had my first Triumph motorcycle. Life was good. But I soon got restless and decided to quit my job to drive to California to be part of the Flower Power scene in San Francisco. I never regretted that decision.

I embraced the hippie philosophy and all that it entailed. To this day, I feel that inside, I am still that hippie with the desire to change the world. I had very long hair, which was standard equipment for hippies. After moving back from San Francisco, I reveled in my life on a 65-acre commune in Maryland. Yes, this hippie lifestyle was much more to my liking than putting up with the corporate world. Cooler people, or so I thought.

Then I got a haircut and that changed everything. I hadn't had a haircut in ages and my long hair started to look a bit too long, if that was possible. Someone at the farm, agreed to give me a haircut. Little did I realize that that my haircutter had her own agenda. When I looked in the mirror after the haircut, most of my long hair was gone. There were no mirrors in the room, so I had no idea of how much she was cutting until there was almost nothing left. Yes, I know that sounds dumb, but that's what happened.

I was now a hippie with short hair. I thought it wouldn't make any difference, as I was still a hippie inside, and I thought that's all that mattered. But it did. I used to get rides by hitchhiking, an event that was quite common and acceptable during the 60s and early 70s. But with my short hair, bus loads of hippies would pass me by and not pick me up. "*Wait,*" I shouted at the VW busses going by, *"I'm a hippie! I just have short hair now.*" No one picked me up. I was too straight looking. Maybe they thought I was a NARC (narcotics officer). That was the worst possible label you could give someone at that time.

I started thinking, hey I'm still a hippie inside. This movement is hypocritical if they judge people simply by the length of their hair. Of course this is quite a generalization, but nevertheless it was my experience. That's not right, I thought. The hippie movement started to make the world a better place, and now it had degenerated into an environment that unless you looked like all the rest of the hippies, you were an outcast. That's why we started wearing our hair long in the first place—to differentiate ourselves from the "straight" people who had jobs, short hair, and who were so uptight (unlike us hippies). "Wait a minute," I thought. We have become the people we were rebelling against. This was too much for me. I decided to search elsewhere for something that I had been looking for—for most of my life. I still had no idea what it was or where to find it. However, I did find what I was seeking in early 1973 thanks to Maharaji. My spiritual life was truly just beginning. But my search was over.

I did go back to work eventually. I finally ended up in the high-tech industry, working for a number of international corporations, traveling the world setting up business deals, and instructing and mentoring MBAs galore, which gave me a sense of pride and accomplishment.

I had only one sibling; Joan, six years younger than me. She was murdered 11 years ago. She married someone I didn't like, and I could never understand my sister's attraction to him, but he had money, thus the initial attraction. They lived in an estate across the street from Paul Newman's home in Westport, Connecticut. Typical story: money, and no happiness, at least towards the end. She lived this life for years, and she was beginning to search for a way out of the mess she had gotten herself into. She didn't have the time to complete the transformation she envisioned, but at least, in her heart, she wanted to make a change. Good for her.

As you can imagine, this shocking event transformed my life as it would transform anyone, although to a much lesser extent than the death of my Evan. After my sister died, I felt as if I needed to think about my life on a more day-to-day basis rather than focus so much on long range plans. Her death was so shocking that I realized that death could come to anyone at anytime. We understand these things intellectually, but when it happens in your home to your family, it's different. It becomes real! However, my realization was only partial in that I wasn't fully cognizant of how important it is to take care of my unfinished business and discover what I need to learn and do.

I also didn't fully put into practice the way I felt about doing things: not putting off the things I wanted to do, and not being stuck doing things I didn't want to do. I had the information in my head, but it wasn't transformed into knowledge via my actions.

The way I reacted to my sister's death was something I couldn't avoid or change. I stopped caring about tomorrow. This attitude certainly effected my job situation because I didn't really care about longevity at one place of employment and that has been somewhat of an issue. I am now resolved that I couldn't help the way I felt and acted. My sister's death was like a mild earthquake, while Evan's death was a catastrophic event. I was jolted by my sister's death and awakened by the death of my Evan.

May 7

I am having trouble writing this because I realize that my future has been completely altered by Evan's death. Without his dying, I think I would have led a fairly unproductive life—not understanding the importance of doing what I needed to do in my remaining years, if I in fact had any years left. More accurate and more pathetic, I knew what was needed to be done and I didn't do it. That statement is completely sad and devastating to me, as it underscores my inherent weakness in the understanding of my purpose and the incredibly sad fact that I had to lose my son to gain myself. I have been avoiding writing this down as it is just too sad for me to deal with, but I wanted this book to be honest and I cannot cheat you or myself by leaving something out. Honesty isn't just telling what you want to tell. A half truth isn't the truth.

There is no measurement possible to calculate the value of getting one's life back on track. Of course I would change it all back to the way it was before I lost Evan in a second, but I can't.

Evan's death has both opened my eyes wider than I thought possible and given me insights into life that I never dreamed I would have or wanted. I am writing these words from a new place. I have seen tomorrow, as death to you, is tomorrow. To me, it is today. In a sense I am trying to describe what happens in a situation like mine so that it can help other people, without them having to go through what I have gone through. When something is clearly given, it must be given back. You can't keep that gift, that's not the purpose of you receiving it. I feel very strongly this is what I am trying to do, through this book.

It's very much like the Dickens Classic, "A Christmas Carol," where the ghost of Christmas future shows Scrooge visions of his future. One day, someone in your family or a friend will die. It's unavoidable. Losing a child brings the deepest pain. They aren't supposed to die before we do. It's unnatural and unthinkable. To me, it is simply amazing that millions of people line up to buy lottery tickets just on the minutest chance that they could win the jackpot, many knowing they are twice as likely to be stuck by lightning than to win the grand prize.

Statistically there are 20 adolescent deaths (ages 5-14) per 100,000 children, according to the latest government statistics. Almost half of those deaths were caused by unintentional accidents. The same statistics also tell us that there are 71 adolescent deaths (ages 15-19) per 100,000 children. It happened in my family, and I couldn't conceive that it could. I knew that I had the slimmest possibility of winning the Powerball lottery, but not the death lottery.

I know what awaits some of you. The suffering, the pain and the regret that is part of the experience when your loved one(s) or friends die is unavoidable. But the regret part, to a certain extent is avoidable. Since we are human, we can not avoid mistakes, and shouldn't feel bad about making them. It's the correcting of improper behavior that we need to be concerned about, before it's too late. You might just think that this is too preachy for your taste; well maybe it is, and maybe it isn't. I can tell you with certainty, there are the usual clichés about making each day count, and always tell your friends and loved ones that you love and care for them. Don't let those things go unsaid. You won't regret it.

Believe me, I thought I knew that "stuff," but looking back, I can see that they were just words that were rambling around in my head along with all that other "stuff" that is supposed to be so important. I wish I knew then what I know now. How often that phrase is repeated! As it is with most things, we think we have all the time in the world to correct our mistakes and learn from the past.

Impact on others:

May 12

I don't think any of us realize the impact we have on other people. Others can judge our impact on them, but we cannot know how much or little impact we have on them. We can't know, and for those who make the greatest impact, it seems they are largely unaware of the ways in which they touch other people's lives. It's probably better that way because our ego would interfere with our actions. The actions wouldn't be for the same purpose, and wouldn't have the same result. I know there are so many people, particularly young people that feel they can't make a difference in this world, after all I'm just one person what can I do? Well, I have seen one person make a huge difference. The impact of Evan's life, and death, is having an effect on a lot of people. Perhaps even you.

At the ceremony for the unveiling of Evan's hockey shirt at the Groton School, I was able to speak for a few minutes. I basically thanked the hockey players for their tribute to Evan then told them about a question that Ryan had been repeating during the weeks after the accident. *"What's the point?"* he kept asking, typically when we were talking about doing something, (oftentimes schoolwork). I could see his point. *"Yeah, what is the point?"* I replied, not having an answer to provide. Evan worked so hard and was so dedicated to achievement, and look what happened to him. I could see why Ryan asked that question.

Then I looked out on the ice and saw all of the hockey teams in full uniform and Evan's friends in the stands. I said *this is the point. "All of you are here to honor Evan and his life, because of the way he lived his life, and because of who he was— that's the point—because he accomplished so much in such a short time.*" If he hadn't tried so hard, he wouldn't have made the transition he made, and the teams wouldn't be honoring him in the way that he has been honored. *That* is the point!

We aren't a finished package until we are finished. We can always alter our package until our time is over. We might look at ourselves and think that we are really a mess, but there is always hope. A snapshot of the early or middle part of Evan's life wouldn't be able to tell the whole story, because he turned everything around at the end of his life, and made the older snapshots irrelevant. An individual picture couldn't sum up his whole life or the future of things to come.

> *"To laugh often and love much; to win the respect of intelligent persons and the affection of children; to earn the approbation of honest citizens and endure the betrayal of false friends; to appreciate beauty; to find the best in others; to give of one's self; to leave the world a bit better, whether by a healthy child, a garden patch or a redeemed social condition; to have played and laughed with enthusiasm and sung with exultation; to know even one life has breathed easier because you have lived—this is to have succeeded."*
> — *Ralph Waldo Emerson*

> *Accompanying the quote was the following:*
>
> *"In many respects, Evan's life must be considered a success. He lived it with zeal and zest and touched countless others. Can any of us ask for more than to live a life of love?"*
> — a Groton resident

Evan's Memorial Service:

Excerpt for a reading selected by Nancy from Kahil Gibran's THE PROPHET

> *And a woman who held a babe against her bosom said, Speak to us of Children*
> *And he said:*
> *Your children are not your children*
> *They are the sons and daughters of Life's longing for itself*
> *They come through you but not from you,*
> *And though they are with you yet they belong not to you.*
> *You may give them your love but not your thoughts,*
> *For they have their own thoughts,*
> *You may house their bodies but not their souls,*
> *For their souls dwell in the house of tomorrow, which you cannot visit, not even in your dreams.*

Ryan's comments:

"Evan was really nice and a respected guy to everybody who knew him. Personally I really miss him a lot. I thought it was really nice how Evan always taught me stuff like how to lift weights and rollerblade, play hockey and pretty much everything else. I also thought his guitar playing was phenomenal. He also taught me how to cradle in lacrosse. Everybody knew my brother and called me little Holofcener. I am really going to miss my brother."

Mark's Eulogy:

"What can I say about my son Evan? That you are loved beyond imagination, and have been since the day you were born. You grew up beautiful, both in body and spirit and had the quest for life found only in true adventurers. Your inquisitive mind challenged the status quo as you should have and you developed your own way, which was important to you.

I remember you as always being cool, way cooler than I ever was or could ever hope to be. You got that from your Mom. As you developed into a young man I started to learn more and more from you and in many ways you inspired me and mentored me, although it should have been the other way around.

You were always so sure of yourself and your sense of being. You were happy with the Evan that you had created from what was originally given you. Your talents were so vast and had such immense potential. I really believed that one day you would be one of those people that could really change the world for the better, either through your music, your art, or your imagination.

You were a wonderful son, a great brother to Ryan and you were just starting to teach Ryan all the things you thought he should know about being cool and making it in middle school. Ryan loved being taught by you. He loved you and always looked up to you because you were his brother, his friend, and his teacher.

Your Mom and you were closer than two people could possibly be. Two bodies in one soul. There was so much of your beautiful mother in you. Your talent, your kindness and your good looks, your empathy, and your ability to figure out just about everything.

I will remember you for your love of music; your learning so many new songs on your awesome Les Paul guitar. Endless hours at Napster, then Morpheus, downloading and downloading songs and trying to figure out how to play them and the joy on your face when you finally got it right.

You were so proud of your muscular body that you worked all summer to perfect. You finally got the six- pack you were striving for, for so long. I think you finally understood that you could achieve anything you wanted to by putting in the effort. You knew you had the core ability to anything you wanted to do and you were just starting to figure that out and it made you feel good about yourself.

You were just figuring out that it was okay to dress preppy sometimes, because clothes don't make you who you are. You were just starting to realize that what you were was inside you, not outside. Clothes didn't matter. It only mattered if someone was nice or not.

I really loved being your dad. I am so proud of everything that you have done. I miss you terribly. I will really miss our bike riding together, I will miss seeing your body being formed to perfection, just the way you wanted it. I will miss not seeing you play in your rock band that you wanted to be in so much. I will miss not seeing your hockey games, where you were getting to become such an awesome force on the rink. I will miss just about everything about you and I hope and pray that you are in a better place and I want you to know that we will love you forever, beyond time and dimensions."

The Epilogue:

May 14

The driver of the truck that struck Evan has now been formally charged with vehicular homicide, driving under the influence of drugs (prescription) and driving to endanger. The case is now being handled by the Superior Court of Massachusetts. Both Nancy and I were at her arraignment, where she was formally charged with Evan's death. It was eerie seeing the person who killed your son. I had no hatred for her, which continues to surprise me, as I thought I would, but I don't. I don't understand why I don't hate this woman, although there are some very strong emotions involved. She is a pathetic creature and her life will be altered for what she did. She will pay for her crime in more ways than just going to jail. I know that hatred leads to suffering, still, I wouldn't mind hating her, but I don't. However, I will leave that option open in the future.

The police have theorized that the woman who was driving the truck was not under control, because of a combination of prescription drugs that she was taking It is also theorized that she probably lost consciousness and wasn't even aware that she struck Evan. That's really pathetic. I hope she will be given a long jail term, but realistically, that most likely won't be the case. I am just beginning to understand that justice is a myth that happens in police dramas on TV, not in real life.

May 15

It's been a little over seven months now. The sympathy cards have stopped coming months ago, along with the calls and people dropping by, except for one loyal friend. It was to be expected. People have gotten on with their lives and they think we are getting along with ours, which we are to a certain extent. We still get a few cards sometimes saying that various people are thinking of us, and most people we meet say they are praying and thinking of us. It seems that Evan's death, like so many other tragedies that happen to other people create a huge wave, then the pond becomes quiet, and people go back to their "normal" lives.

Knowing what I know now, I wouldn't like to have a "normal" life at all because a normal life is typically one where we don't question our purpose on earth, and live in a state of forgetfulness of our true purpose. It's similar to the September 11th tragedy. People have moved on and their lives are unchanged for the most part. The people who lost loved ones feel differently. It truly isn't possible to comprehend with your mind what losing a child does to you. I am doing the best I can to provide information based on my experience. Hopefully this can help anyone to move forward in their evolutionary path, without having to go through a tragedy, or minimally, to get you to think about life in a manner that is not consistent with your past. That would make me very happy. I know it would also make Evan very happy as well.

Never in a billion, trillion years did I think that Evan wouldn't be around every morning, at least until he went away to college. Each and every day I would come into the kitchen in the morning and he would be there, and we would pass the time together. I never thought it would turn out this way, but it did.

The pain was actually increasing each and every day for the first few months, as the initial protective shock started to wear off. The anti-depressants that Nancy and I are both taking kicked in 30 days from the time you are first prescribed them. Thank God for antidepressants; they really are quite helpful. I don't really want to take them forever, but for now, they are saving me from even more pain, and that doesn't seem so bad. Evan's death is more real now, and that is something I did not anticipate. It's a lot like anesthesia wearing off from a major invasive operation: the pain hits you like….. actually I cannot describe it. If I could somehow describe it, you probably wouldn't be able to understand it anyway. At Compassionate Friends meetings other parents have said the second year is worse than the first. A few months ago I thought that statement was inconceivable. How could anything be worse than the first year? But now, I can see where that might actually be true. Time does heal, but time also makes the loss more real too.

May 18

When people see us they always ask *"how are you doing?"* I get the distinct feeling that they expect that we are doing much better now. It doesn't work that way. There is just no way that people can comprehend that we will never get completely better. Do they think we are *over* Evan and that our lives are back to normal? Our lives will *never* be normal. When people have diseases there is always the hope that they will recover and everything will return to normal. The hope, even the faintest glimmer of hope that you will get better makes things livable to a certain extent. With death, there is no hope. It's something you get through, not over.

May 20

One awful experience I go through everyday is looking at Evan's photographs, which are everywhere in our house. It seems like a dream that he was in our family. It is getting harder and harder to remember his physical presence. It's like a picture that is slowly going out of focus when you desperately want it to be crystal clear. More than that, I want Evan to be with me so I don't have to look at a picture to see him, but it is not to be.

We made it through our first Thanksgiving and Christmas without Evan. We went away for both vacations— to a friend's house for Thanksgiving and to Nancy's Dad's house for Christmas— which gave us a chance to see her brother and nephews. It felt good getting out of town and being with friends and family, but each holiday found us very sad on the trip home, thinking about not having Evan with us and knowing that never again will we be able to celebrate anything with him physically.

We had a beautiful celebration for him on January 9th, his birthday. Close friends of his and close friends of ours dropped by the house to celebrate Evan's life. We showed videos of Evan, and all of us were transfixed at seeing him again, albeit in a video. There were many, many tears shed. We sang "Happy Birthday" and each person wrote a note to Evan and sent it to the heavens tied to a helium balloon. There was a lot of excitement and awe at being able to send heartfelt messages to him, even though it was symbolic. The sense of connection to Evan at that time was quite strong and quite real.

We received a few notes on his birthday, which were quite touching:

> *"Just a little something in loving remembrance, thanks, and honor of the beautiful soul that was entrusted to you; and who continues to bless the lives of so many he encountered in this realm."*
> *— a neighborhood mom*

> *"Evan, I think about you at least several times a day. I hope that you would be pleased to know that we now view you as a role model to demonstrate devotion, dedication, and "passion" for yourself and all who knew you."*
> *— a neighborhood mom*

May 23

I went for a bike ride on the hardest trail I know, a trail Evan and I called "The Triangle." We rode this trail together many, many times during last summer. I was laid off from my high tech job in June so we were able to spend the entire summer bike riding and hanging out. We were both in the best physical shape we could remember. I was trying so hard to keep up with Evan on that trail. Just as I was about to catch up with him he would look back at me (as he was always in the lead), and give me "the smile" and take off as if he were rocket-propelled. I would yell out at him and he would turn around and give me an even broader smile. He was letting me catch up with him all along, just to make me feel good. Now, he has really gone on ahead and I wonder if I will ever catch up with him. My bike rides are so lonely now. It will never be the same.

Incidentally, I will *never* go back to my high tech job. Writing is now what I intend to do, and I will try and relate my experiences throughout the rest of my life in hopes that they may be of some help. I hope my writing gets better, but it will always be truthful and real and hopefully inspiring.

May 24

One major concern I had was the thought that Evan would be able to perceive pain when he was hit. I didn't think so, because he was stuck so suddenly, and the driver was going about approximately 35 miles an hour. Evan really flew when he rode, so the impact would have been "*very* sudden. I was haunted by the thought that he could have known what was happening to him, even for a brief second. It was a deeply troubling thought and I couldn't get it out of my mind.

About a month after Evan's death, I went through a really angry period. I was angry with everything. One day, I was so pissed off that I had to go bike riding just to relieve my anger. I biked on the rail trail near our house that had just been completed. I was going quite fast as the madder I was the harder I biked. It was the first week in October and I was wearing new biking gloves. At one point my nose began to run I slowly took off one glove to search for a tissue in my pocket. I started to drift toward the edge of the rail trail, and the next thing I knew, I was on the ground bleeding quite profusely from my chin.

Fortunately there was a police cruiser nearby that showed up about 30 seconds later in a desolate spot on the rail trail, where I was laying on the ground. I noticed it was the same crew who responded to Evan's accident. They told me I had a rather nasty cut on my chin, which eventually required eleven stitches. I was taken to the nearby hospital where Evan was initially taken.

The good thing about my bike accident was that I have no memory of the time when I fell down and hit my chin on the pavement. The last thing I remember was drifting toward the edge of the trail. My glasses were scratched, my jacket had a rip in the back, my chin was bleeding, and my gloves were torn, yet I had no memory of falling and hitting my chin until I was lying on the ground. I don't know how anything occurred, even though I was going relatively slow. I didn't feel any pain whatsoever, until about 15 minutes after I hit my chin, as the protective shock took over, preventing me from feeling the pain. I must have been only going about 10 mph when my accident occurred. That was when I realized that Evan never knew or felt anything when he was hit. I instantly felt better about the thoughts that were haunting me and causing me so much torment. They vanished for good.

When I think back to my accident, I am grateful for having it because it helped me through a difficult time. It made me realize that Evan transitioned from an earthly body to a spirit in the blink of an eye, with no pain or awareness.

May 26

"Fountain Will Memorialize a 'Truly Gifted Child,'" read the headlines in the *Public Spirit*, a local newspaper.

Wonderful neighbors of ours, Donna and her daughter Amanda, have worked very hard to create a lasting and appropriate tribute to Evan. A portion of the Rail-Trail, which is being built through Groton will be dedicated to Evan. The town of Groton will install a water fountain, which will become a rest stop, in his memory. The architect is working with our family on a suitable design. Evan would be happy as he spent a lot of time on that trail, especially before it was paved, and he really loved to ride his bike.

May 29

My need to reach out and try and do something with young people has taken on quite a significance in my life since Evan's death. The feeling is definitely one of need as opposed to want. I have to take care of those feelings because they are so strong and consistent with what I know and feel is my new life's work. It's as if I have an obligation to help, as I know I can now be of assistance. I have a strong feeling that Evan would want me to continue to try and help his friends and other kids, as he was starting to do. I do now what I *must do.*

I feel wonderful when I do something that I know Evan would want me to do. Sure, it's speculation on my part, as there is no scientific evidence that Evan is involved, but there is a feeling that I have that I don't really have to justify to anyone.

People have been asking me who this book is for, and I could never answer them, since I never thought about writing this book in the first place. It just happened. Initially, there were mixed messages in the book, some toward teenagers, some toward parents and others toward everyone else. As of January, 2002, I still didn't know who the book was being written for and didn't care; but I wondered why all of the adults who were reading the rough draft kept asking the same question.

When adults would read the rough draft, they would want me to reorganize the book in a more orderly fashion, something I wasn't opposed to, since I am not the most orderly person to begin with. Some of the adults thought the book was good, but that was about it. I kept asking *"how did you feel after reading the draft*?" I wanted people to get something from this book that can change their life, not simply read it and move on, or move backward, or not move at all.

The teenagers were another story. The teenagers seemed to "get it." As more adults were shown the draft they too were getting it as I began changing the focus. Something curious began to happen. A good proportion of the adults reading the draft mentioned that they were changing some aspects of their life that they had wanted to change for a long time. They were actually doing it! It made me quite happy, and I certainly understand their change of heart.

The following is an email I received from a schoolmate of Evan's who had been having trouble with depression. I gave this person a rough draft to read, to see what, if anything, they got out of it.

"I' m just writing to say how completely awesome your book is. Ever since I got the rough draft I've kept reading, and re reading this incredible work. The hardest part for me was when it was over."

This poem was written in the same email. It is considerably different in a good way from their previous poetry. It's the first positive poem I have seen from this person

"Life is a search
For happiness and bliss
What is it?
Where is it?
Can it be found?
In money?
In fame?
Or maybe in a kiss?
I've been searching endlessly
To find my own spiritual joy
But society forbids me
Taunts me, pulls me, and bends me like a toy
I am forced to hide under the masks
Which Evan hated so
Sometimes my body wants to stay
But my mind needs to go
Go to someplace where everything is better
I can be whoever I want
Without being shadowed by pain and stormy weather
This place may only exist in thought
But at least I can be thirsty enough to be determined to find a person, place thing or belief, that will grant me true happiness.

Up until now I was sure such a place could not exist. I was too enthralled with my own self demise to realize I can be truly happy, that life really is worth living. Evan found the joy in all that he did. He had the power to help, and heal anyone who needed it. Sometimes they didn't even ask, he just knew. He "just knew" a lot of things, and people trusted him, more than they would trust any other soul. For a lot of people Evan brought true happiness to their lives. It makes me wonder if there is more than one "true happiness", if so, would it or could it be like Evan? I hope someday to have the answers to these questions. Until then,

> *I search and search, and search. Thank you for setting me in the right direction."*

When I read this beautiful email, I was happy that I trusted my inner feelings enough to write this book. If it is only for this one person, then it will have been worth all the effort.

Great news! I talked with Chuck White about the fund set up for the Hockey Scholarship. I was feeling that I didn't want one or two players to benefit from the money. After all the whole team dedicated their season to Evan. I had an idea. Chuck went for it. The entire Bantam 2 hockey team will be going to a rock concert with their dads, courtesy of Evan. As I am writing this I have a *huge* smile on my face. I had almost forgotten what a smile feels like.

Interesting happenings

June 1

I remember we spent the night in Buffalo, New York on our way to Christmas in Michigan. It was just before the record snowfall hit. I was awakened twice that night by a bright shining light in our room in the shape of a star. I was completely awake at the time. I wasn't exactly sure what was going on, but it was totally cool. I was just amazed that this event occurred. Nancy said it was a spirit. The sight I witnessed, she said, has been described in various books that she is reading as the true form of a spirit.

There are people that do have some answers about death, from their years of research including Dr. Elisabeth Kübler-Ross, or Brian Moody, that have spent decades dealing with near death experiences (NDE). They have come to the conclusion that we live on after death in the spirit world, learning our lessons and preparing for our next life here on earth. There are also the experiences of Dr. Brian Weiss regarding past-life regression, which essentially, through the experiences of his patients, comes to virtually the same conclusions about life, death, and our journey to completion. You may or may not believe in any of their theories. There is however, a compelling case that is being made for a life after death as a spirit, living and growing in the spirit world.

In November of 2001, Nancy met with Rev. Simeon Stefanidakis of the First Spiritual Temple, located in Brookline, Massachusetts. He is a well renowned medium—someone who channels the spirits of departed souls. Nancy had been plagued with the question about Evan being okay, even though he was dead. Was he okay? That's all she wanted to know, and I knew she would do everything and anything she could to find the answer, as is typical for her. To that end, Nancy now has an enormous collection of books on death and dying, and is continually expanding the number of authors she reads and respects. The books help her to get a perspective from various sources to either validate or invalidate her feelings about death and the afterlife, and to enhance her earthly education about the spirit world.

During her session with the medium, it seemed that Nancy did in fact make contact with Evan. As it wasn't my experience, I can't comment on it directly, only as a third party. Nancy did feel as though the connection was made. She knows, by the way the medium described Evan, his departure from this earth, and his mannerisms. The medium only knew Nancy's first name and nothing about our family or anything about Evan and the accident.

I did listen to a tape of the session and found it pretty interesting, to say the least. Through the medium, Evan said that *"he was whole now, and that he was okay*." He said *"he would have done some things differently and listened to some people more,*" and that *"he was having a good time there, better than here."* He also said *"that he would be the first person to meet Nancy when she passed into the spirit world."*

Regardless of what you may think about mediums, Nancy felt better knowing that Evan was okay. That is what is important. Nancy continues to amaze me with her devotion to finding out more about the spiritual world and has just signed up to take mediumship classes to enable her to be a medium, so that she can stay connected to Evan throughout her life. I too have signed up and we both just graduated from the course. After experiences in the mediumship classes, we both have decided to continue our studies in this field. I can only say that the mediumship classes were incredible, *"way* beyond my expectations. I actually felt and perceived something not from this physical world. I have sensed the spirits of deceased people and given accurate interpretations of those people to the other people in the classes, making the readings verifiable.

I too had a session with Rev. Simeon Stefanidakis, and *definitely* connected to Evan. How do I know? A father knows his son. The session was so overwhelming that I could barely remember anything that was said. I am glad the session was taped. Evan told me of his love for me and that we would continue to work on our relationship once I was in the spirit world. Interesting enough, my father also was present, much to my annoyance. He is gone and still can't leave me alone. He kept saying he was sorry.

Nancy and I each visited the Weiss Institute in Miami in early 2002, and we were both hypnotized and past life-regressed. Our experiences were extraordinary but different. Nancy went back into past lives which helped her to understand why this life was progressing the way it has. I went into the spirit world and spent an hour being with Evan. My feeling upon entering the spirit world is beyond my ability to truly describe. Everything was gone, all worries, fears and doubts. It was as if I was in the midst of the entire universe. Then all of a sudden I was feeling lost until I heard Evan calling me. *"Hey Dad, come here I want to show you something really cool."* Initially I had been in complete darkness but when Evan called me to him, I was transported to a place of beautiful light. I was mesmerized. Once my session was over I expressed my surprise at going to the spirit world instead of going into a past life, to the therapist. She said *"you always get what you need. It's always perfect."*

It was perfect. Evan mentioned a number of things concerning this book, which made me feel *REALLY GOOD*!

Both the experience with the medium and the past life regression session were consistent with my old and new nature. Experience things for yourself, so you don't have to believe anyone or anything. I have experienced things in the last seven months that I never dreamed were possible. I will continue to seek out new experiences and report on them. I am doing this for myself, but if it can help anyone else, then we will both benefit.

June 3

In April of 2002, Nancy was attending an Omega Institute convention in New York City. During one session James Van Praagh, a well know medium and author, recently featured in a TV mini-series, asked anyone in the audience of well over 500 if they were recently taking care of an older gentleman in a wheelchair— a father figure. He was specifically pointing to the section where Nancy was seated. Two people stood up, one being Nancy. He then asked who was recently looking through old family photographs. Only Nancy was left standing. The medium was receiving messages from my father. Actually, this was the fourth time my father has communicated to either Nancy or me via a medium. It's the same message every time. He told Nancy how sorry he was for the way he acted during his life. Nancy said *"he should be."* But it's too late now! Both Nancy and I expressed our thoughts about the probability of his regret for so many things that he did when he was alive, but he wouldn't listen. I now have a good idea of what my Dad may have been trying to say to Nancy minutes before he died. Both Nancy and I have forgiven my father, and wish him well in his new surroundings.

Everything that has been happening since Evan's death is leading me to both know and accept that there is much more to this life than I could possibly have imagined. That is both wonderful and exciting, if you are the adventurous kind. I know beyond a shadow of a doubt that there is life after this one. Because of that, my life has changed, as it should. I am now doing those things that I need do to in this life to complete my mission successfully. The cloud will still be over me, but you can imagine how good it feels to know your life's purpose and the way to experience true love. What more could I want. I still want Evan, and I don't imagine that will ever stop. I do *know* that we will meet up again, and continue our lives together. And the best part is that it's not a belief.

Evan really did have a wonderful adventure here on earth. The greatest adventure I ever witnessed. I am so happy that he that he was able to fulfill his dreams of living an adventurous life and doing the best he could in his allotted time. With the exception of a few rough spots, he had a ball. He is now on the greatest adventure of all time—and the adventure continues.

Parents Report Card

The Parent's Report Card © is meant to be a guideline for discussion within a family. This idea came to me one day and I immediately wrote it down. I know that children, especially younger children have a hard time verbalizing their thoughts. This report card is a way for them to grade their parents. Typically, it is the other way around. I thought the children should have a voice that needs be heard, and hopefully this vehicle can help.

It may be easier to have the children pick 5 topics each week and incorporate them into a family meeting rather than have them answer all the questions at once. Of course this will also be dependent on the ages of the children. This list of questions can be expanded upon, as each family is unique and can compose questions more pertinent to your family's needs. The importance of this report card is that it is giving the children a voice, where they may have had none. Keep their answers sacred.

Parents Report Card©

Key for Grading:

A= Makes me feel good

B= I like that

C= it's just OK

D= I don't like that child grades Discussion Date

F= Makes me feel bad parent Needed Solution

Parents Report Card©			
Action(s)	**Child Grades Parent**	**Discussion Needed**	**Date Solution**
Key for Grading: ***A** = Makes me feel good* ***B** = I like that* ***C** = it's just OK* ***D** = I don't like that child grades Discussion Date* ***F** = Makes me feel bad parent Needed Solution*			
Shows love, kisses, hugs, hold hands,etc when appropriate. Not afraid to show me they love me			
Respects me, treats me like I am worth listening to			
Yells at me instead of talking with me			
Is mean to me a lot for no reason			
Punishes me without good reason			
Listens to me when I want to talk			
Stays away when I want them to			
Trusts me-believes what I say			

Parents Report Card©			
Action(s)	**Child Grades Parent**	**Discussion Needed**	**Date Solution**
Key for Grading: ***A** = Makes me feel good* *__B__ = I like that* *__C__ = it's just OK* ***D** = I don't like that child grades Discussion Date* ***F** = Makes me feel bad parent Needed Solution*			
Talks to me about important things like happiness, real success, not just school, sports, or grades.			
Lectures me, doesn't talk to me			
Makes me do everything their way—doesn't let me do things my way			
Goes on dates with me, doing things I want to do			
Encourages me and lets me know what I am doing right or wrong, so that I can do a better job next time			

Parents Report Card©			
Action(s)	**Child Grades Parent**	**Discussion Needed**	**Date Solution**
Key for Grading: ***A** = Makes me feel good* *__B__ = I like that* *__C__ = it's just OK* ***D** = I don't like that child grades Discussion Date* ***F** = Makes me feel bad parent Needed Solution*			
Trains/instructs me on how to do stuff: water lawn, pot plants, do dishes, set the table, fold laundry, change bike tire, cook meals that I am able, pour milk, juices, how to type, make my bed, clean my room			
Lets me do for myself what I know how to do- not to it for me, like making my lunch, making my bed, recycling			
Helps me with my homework/jobs without losing their temper or making me feel stupid			
Hurts my feelings, makes me feel bad about myself and my ability to do things			
Understands that I am not an adult and I will make mistakes sometimes, and that is OK.			

Parents Report Card©

Action(s)	Child Grades Parent	Discussion Needed	Date Solution
Key for Grading: ***A*** *= Makes me feel good* ***B*** *= I like that* ***C*** *= it's just OK* ***D*** *= I don't like that child grades Discussion Date* ***F*** *= Makes me feel bad parent Needed Solution*			
If I try my hardest and fail you get mad at me and make me feel bad			
Does what they say we shouldn't do, like drinking soda and saying we shouldn't drink it.			
Follows through on what they say they are going to do			
Encourages me to try my hardest and doesn't get mad if I don't do my best			
Talks to me about spiritual things			
Accepts me for who and what I am—I am not like everyone else			
Has a good sense of humor—is fun to be around			

Parents Report Card©

Action(s)	Child Grades Parent	Discussion Needed	Date Solution
Key for Grading: ***A** = Makes me feel good* ***B** = I like that* ***C** = it's just OK* ***D** = I don't like that child grades Discussion Date* ***F** = Makes me feel bad parent Needed Solution*			
Helps me to understand the real meaning of success-relationships, deeds, kindness, character, charity or volunteer work, not just having a lot of money.			
Takes time to talk me about my day, my friends, what's happened during school, if I want to talk			
Uses TV to baby sit me instead of playing or talking with me			
Makes me do things I don't want to do like play sports or piano			
Doesn't let me take piano or play sports that I want to do			
Always makes up with me before the end of the day—no matter who is at fault			

Parents Report Card©			
Action(s)	**Child Grades Parent**	**Discussion Needed**	**Date Solution**
Key for Grading: ***A** = Makes me feel good* ***B** = I like that* ***C** = it's just OK* ***D** = I don't like that child grades Discussion Date* ***F** = Makes me feel bad parent Needed Solution*			
Lets me make mistakes, like breaking a dish when letting me try to do the dishes and not getting mad.			
Jumps to conclusions about who is guilty before getting facts when we fight with our brothers or sisters			

Evan's Earthly Adventure
Order Form

Each copy of Evan's Earthly Adventure is $13.00 plus $3.00 shipping per book

My check or money order for $________________________ is enclosed

Massachusetts residents add 5% sales tax per book. Please allow 7 days for delivery.

If you wish to use a credit card please check the website: www.evansearthlyadventure.com

Name____

Address____

City, State, ZIP____

Please make your checks payable to
BeyondTime Books
P.O. Box 930
Groton, MA 01450
www.evanearthlyadventure.com